Fair Seed-Time
William Crackanthorpe
His Irish & Grand Tours
in Napoleonic Wartime
1812-1815

Other Books by David Crackanthorpe

Novels

Stolen Marches
Horseman Pass By
The Ravenglass Line
This time the Flames
The Seventh Clause

Biographies

Hubert Crackanthorpe & English Realism in the 1890s
Bruffam a life of Henry Brougham

Travel & History

Marseille
The Camisard Uprising

Topography & History

Pele Towers of the Eden Valley

Copyright: David Crackanthorpe
First edition 2024
ISBN 978-1-912181-68-1
Published by Bookcase, 19 Castle St., Carlisle, CA3 8SY
01228 544560 bookscumbria@aol.com
Printed by The Amadeus Press.

Fair Seed-Time:
William Crackanthorpe
Irish & Grand Tours
in Napoleonic Wartime
1812-1815

edited by David Crackanthorpe

BOOKCASE

*William Crackanthorpe (1820) by Henry Raeburn
Dumfries House: Mount Stuart Trust.*

Contents

Introduction by David Crackanthorpe   **7**

Part I: 1812   **17**

Belfast, Coleraine, Giants Causeway, Londonderry, Strabane, Donegall, Sligo. Westport, 17-32; Tuam, Galway, Dromoland, Moher, Tralee.34-49; Limerick, Killarney, Bantry, Cork, 41-49; Clonmel, Desart, Kilkenny, Vinegar Hill, 52-54; Glendalough, Dublin, 55-58.

Part II : 1813-1814   **61**

Harwich, Gothenburgh, 59-71; Ystadt, Brandenburgh, 76; Stralsund, Berlin, Potsdam, 79-82; Leipzig, Frankfort, Hanau, 90-99; Stutgard, 107-118; Black Forest, 119; Schafhausen, 120; Munich, 122-128; Vienna *January – May 1814*; Pressburg, Neusohl, 153-157; Gratz, 158; Fiume, 159; Trieste, 161; Venice *July 1814*, 163-166; Florence, 167; Elba, 169-172; Florence, 175-178; Milan, 179; Genoa, 183; Florence, 186; Rome *December 1814*, 188-200; Naples *Feb. 1814*, 201-207; Rome *April 1814*, 208; Florence, *April 1815*, 209-215; Munich, Vienna *June 1815*, 215-217;.Paris. *August 1815*, 220-225; Brussels, Waterloo *September 1815*, 226; London, 227.

Epilogue   **229**

*William aged 8 in 1798.
H & M Sawrey-Cookson.*

Introduction

William Crackanthorpe was born in 1790, a year after the outbreak of the French Revolution. In 1800, on the death of his father, he inherited Newbiggin Hall near Temple Sowerby in Westmorland. Until his majority, the estate was managed by his mother and she continued her watch during his time of travels. ('Your judgement is better than mine in these affairs,' he wrote). He had two sisters, Charlotte and Sarah, who remained all their lives at Newbiggin.

William was educated at Sedbergh until fourteen, then at the fashionable house of Dr. Gretton in Windsor, known for its easy-going regime. He went on to St John's College, Cambridge, where his cousin, William Wordsworth, had preceded him, and where many of his lasting friendships were made.

These naturally tended to be with other young men of independent means. Although the Newbiggin estate, whose core at Newbiggin proceeded from a grant of 1150, was not rich compared to those of some of his friends, it was enough to ensure him a choice of life. But the property as a whole, and Newbiggin Hall in particular, were suffering from long neglect since the death of James Crackanthorpe, William's great-uncle, in 1752; and although his father Christopher had begun the process of repair in the late 18th century it was incomplete when he died. Drawings show a part of the house which had been damaged in the Wars of the Roses and reconstructed in the mid-16th century as semi-ruinous in 1840.

Nevertheless it was with relative advantages that at the age of twenty-two William set out on the first of his travels, taking

Newbiggin Hall, south front, circa 1800.

him round Ireland where his friend Lord Sligo owned a much larger estate and a fine 18th century mansion at Westport, Co. Mayo. The two friends would a year later join together to make the Grand Tour, from Sweden to Italy and finally to Paris, regardless of the ongoing Napoleonic war with its battles and movement of armies, maritime blockade and universal civil oppression.

There were some marked differences of personality between the two men, though they seem to have travelled together for the better part of three years in perfect companionship. William was raised as a modest north-country squire of old stock, not a fashionable dandy (or *petit maître,* an expression used by Sligo

Newbiggin Hall, the north part in ruinous condition

to his mother). He appeared, at the outset, comparatively unworldly though fond of society, and still gifted with a fresh keenness of observation. Sligo, two years his senior, lived already on the fringe of the Prince Regent's band of followers, and was familiar since childhood with Court circles since his mother, a daughter of the naval hero Admiral Lord Howe, had long been in favour with King George III and his family. Sligo, inheriting his father's title of Marquess with a great fortune, was therefore very much a young man of the world. He had already travelled round the Mediterranean and in Greece, sometimes in company with Byron; he had fathered a child with a young woman kept as mistress, on and off, in Paris; and he had been in trouble with the

*Lord Sligo by William Beechey.
Westport House*

law for inducing naval seamen in Malta to desert their post and join the crew of a sloop-of-war rented for his escapades in the Aegean. In short, this early part of his adult life — to become much steadier before long —had a decidedly rakish and extravagant style. His inclination was to follow adventure in the wake of the allied armies as they forced their way westward across Europe and eventually to Paris in victory. William's inclination was towards improvement of his knowledge of languages and the arts, particularly in Italy. They were both horrified by what they saw of the consequences of war as they made their way through Germany, but Sligo was ready to follow the armies further; William, whose French sympathies seemed to increase as he became older, became also more pacific the more familiar he grew with the peaceful arts of Europe in their birthplace.

Accordingly, after a winter spent in Vienna they separated for a time, joining up again in the spring of 1815 in Rome, Naples, and later in Paris. Meanwhile, Sligo's place as William's *compagnon de voyage* on the onward journey from Vienna was taken by another former college friend, Lord Dumfries, who, on November 16th 1814, was to succeed his grandfather as 2nd Marquess of Bute. The contrast between Sligo and Dumfries could hardly have been greater. Sligo was accepted and indulged as a sower of wild oats suited to his age. Dumfries was more solemn, and judged then and later as somewhat dour, focussed less on social pleasures than on increasing his fortune from the South Wales coal fields and construction of the Cardiff docks. But William saw much to admire in him, and for some time after their return worked with him on management of the estate on the Isle of Bute — at least until the Westmorland election of 1820, the year in which Henry Raeburn's portrait of William in Dumfries House was commissioned.

*Lord Bute by Henry Raeburn
Mount Stuart Trust*

Henry Peter Brougham by Thomas Lawrence, 1825

William was a confirmed Whig from an early age — 'Brougham-ish in politics' in Sligo's phrase. He was an active supporter of Henry Brougham in his attempts on the Westmorland parliamentary seat in famously close-run elections of 1818 and 1820, regarded then and later as the first shift towards parliamentary reform, and he remained all his life prominent in Whig politics in Cumbria. He was nominated Whig candidate for Westmorland at the first general election after the passing of the Reform Act of 1832, but this remained a Tory seat. However, his involvement in so hotly contested a political period would unavoidably distance him from markedly Tory friends such as Bute, a passionate opponent of electoral reform of which one of the leading advocates was Brougham.

Notwithstanding these potential differences the group of fortunate young men, and others mentioned in the letters and diary, took their chance and their luck together in this closing phase of the Napoleonic era with all its drama, excitement and hope.

Note on the Text

This is composed from William's diaries in Ireland in 1812, from his diary on the continental tour of 1813-1815, and from extracts out of the 50 letters addressed to his mother and sisters at Newbiggin during his travels. These first appeared serialised in "The Penrith Observer" in 1891, under the editorship of Daniel Scott.

The collection as a whole was auctioned at Christies in June 1992, and is now held by the University of Cambridge Library. Included with it were numerous letters and folded notes, most of them (in Christie's slightly prim phrasing), 'from young ladies.' These were usually written in French and addressed to William as *gentilhomme anglais* wherever he was lodged.

The letters from Sligo to his mother, from which extracts are quoted, are held in Maynooth University Library.

Editorial notes and contextual additions appear in italics within the text. The place of excisions is indicated by a triple stop, thus: …

Acknowledgements

My thanks are due to Westport House for the image of Sir William Beechey's portrait of Howe Peter Browne 2nd Marquess of Sligo; and for permission to reproduce it.

I am grateful to the Mount Stuart Trust for permission to reproduce: Henry Raeburn. William Crackanthorpe, 1820. Oil on canvas on loan at Dumfries House from the Bute Collection at Mount Stuart; and Henry Raeburn. John Crichton-Stuart, 2nd Marquess of Bute, 1821. Oil on canvas. The Bute Collection at Mount Stuart.

The miniature portrait of William Crackanthorpe as a boy on page 1 is now in the collection of H. & M. Sawrey-Cookson to whom I am indebted for its use here.

Stephen Pope's *Cassell Dictionary of Napoleonic Wars,* with more than 1,000 entries, has been an encyclopaedic resource for wartime context, detail, and chronology.

Grateful acknowledgement to Simon Ledingham for photos on pp. 4,6,8,9,229 and 232 and particularly for that of Henry Raeburn's portrait of William Crackanthorpe at Dumfries House which provides the cover and frontispiece.

The title, 'Fair Seed-Time', is taken from *The Prelude* by William Wordsworth, bk.1 line 300.

My grateful thanks, as always, to my wife Laura for essential help.

David Crackanthorpe

Ireland: Places mentioned on the tour

PART I
Ireland 1812

William set off from Newbiggin in the early summer of 1812, intending to travel round the country nearest to the Atlantic coast from Belfast to Dublin. He sailed from Stanraer to Larne and thence to Belfast, observing its situation: —

"peculiarly favourable for American and West Indian commerce ... its loch one of the finest harbours perhaps in the world in which ships of the largest burden can ride at all times with the greatest safety. I saw it indeed under circumstances by no means favourable, as the day was very wet & in consequence of the Assizes at Downpatrick the inn very uncomfortable. I determined therefore to proceed immediately, but as there were no horses to be got ... I was under the necessity of changing my route and going by the mail to Coleraine, instead of pursuing the line of coast, which was my original intention ... We proceeded to Ballymory and afterwards to Coleraine without seeing anything worthy of remark except numbers of round green low mounds, supposed to be Danish forts or Druidical monuments. These are very numerous throughout the whole of the north of Ireland and like the round towers which everywhere present themselves, have puzzled all the researches of Antiquarians & outlived all the tales of tradition."

The particular archaeological interest of the Irish megalithic burial mounds – the most famous being those at New Grange and the Bend of the Boyne – was much written about in the mid-19th century by Sir William Wilde (father of Oscar), among others.

Coleraine

View of the Old Bridge in Coleraine, 1843

But until the publication, a century after William Crackanthorpe's tour, of the work of George Coffey, Keeper of Irish Antiquities in the National Museum, it was not widely known. Mysterious mounds and stone circles continued to be ascribed to the Druids whose history was often a focus of popular delusion.

"Coleraine is a neat small town upon the river bank, in the county of Derry, the manor & living being under the jurisdiction of the Corporation of the city of London. It is the great resort of travellers visiting the giants causeway, from whom & the great fishery, which produces many thousands a year, the principal part of its wealth is derived, that of the salmon being let for £6000 & the eel for £1000. The fish of course is not all consumed here but exported in fast sailing smacks to Liverpool, being first packed up in ice. It was about ten o'clock in the evening when we arrived here, & with some difficulty having been furnished with beds, as the house was very full, I next morning, of course, made all due enquiries, what means I should employ to go and see this

Giant's Causeway. 1854

stupendous work of nature, & following the recommendation of my good landlady I hired a car (or an Irish vis à vis on which the passengers sit back to back), on which I went to Bushmills, & having procured a guide, one Alexander McMullen, an extremely sensible, shrewd & intelligent fellow, I proceeded to view the giants causeway."

William's curiosity about all he saw showed a marked visual sensibility open to the Romantic inclinations of his time and their vocabulary. Sublimity and the sublime feature largely among otherwise precise descriptions of scenes whose impression he hoped to remember, the work of natural forces surpassing the creative abilities of mankind.

"And, now, I would that I had a pen which could describe or a pencil which could delineate in any way, however faint, so

Giant's Causeway

magnificent and wonderful an object; I know not, indeed, whether the imposing grandeur of the headlands, or the beautiful and exquisite precision of the causeway is more worthy of admiration & much do I pity the want of feeling in those (& many I am told there are) who return, after seeing them, disappointed. The causeway is a mole extending between three & four hundred yards into the sea composed of regular basaltic columns and by some has been compared to a honeycomb, to which it bears a striking resemblance, except that the forms all are hexagonal, being a figure next to a circle of the greatest capacity, whilst these vary in their number of sides from three to nine. Each of these pillars also consists of separate pieces of different lengths fitted to each other in the most compact manner, for wherever the base of the one is convex, the head of the other is concave & so the reverse, whilst a kind of curb ... runs up at each angle, thus rendering them almost inseparable. But the most singular phenomenon perhaps are the Whynn Dikes, vast basalt walls cutting perpendicularly the face of the precipices, at the bottom of which they lose themselves in the sea ... These are all composed of various sized horizontal prisms, but generally of a finer nature of basalt than the columns the prisms of which are all vertical, that divide, as it were, this grand and sublime piece of architecture into different compartments varying in their length from 10 or 12 feet to a few inches. The two great promontories of Benbane and Fairhead are the most striking feature on this coast, between which there are numerous capes composed of ranges of pillars resting upon different strata; but of these Blaskin is by far the most conspicuous. Here are two ranges of the columnar basalt each of which is sixty feet high built with all the regularity which art could have bestowed intersected by a range of coarse rock of nearly equal thickness. These two galleries about 170 feet in height resting upon another rock which is nearly

200 feet more, form a precipice unequalled in grandeur & beauty to any other in the world.

After having staid here between six & seven hours (and it would require as many days to satisfy my curiosity) I walked on to meet my car two or three miles along the coast, in order that it might carry me on to Carrick a Rede, where there is a most curious bridge formed of ropes between the main land and a small island. This is made for the convenience of the fishermen during the summer months but I do not think that all the salmon in the world would induce me to cross it once ... yet I saw a poor old man of 78 with only one leg trip over it as lightly and unconcernedly as if it had been iron. Only one accident however hath yet been known to have occurred, which I think can only be looked upon as a miracle when we consider, that it is made only of three ropes attached at each end to three rings fastened in the rocks and kept at equal distances by pieces of wood thro' which the ropes pass and then covered with thin deal boards extending in length nearly 60 feet and above 70 from the water below.

The next day I again hired the same vehicle & went down to call upon Dr Richardson, a man well known to the literary and agricultural world by his geological and botanical researches. To him we are indebted for many new discoveries, which tend to throw some light upon the formation of the causeway or rather to overthrow the theories of the vulcanists & those who maintain that it is a volcanic production ..."

William Richardson, 1740-1820, DD and former Fellow of University College Dublin, was a clergyman and a prolific pamphleteer. His alternative arguments to those of the vulcanists on the origin of the basalt columns were finally disproved but his agricultural theories on winter hay production and the drainage of peat bogs for reducing the poverty of tenant farmers throughout Ireland remained historically most influential.

"To him also is the farmer indebted for the fiorin grass ... in which should he succeed ... we have found a greater benefactor to the world than in all the agriculturalists of the last century. Having presented my credentials, he immediately came out to me, insisted upon the return of my vehicle & that I should remain a few days with him in order that he might shew me the numberless curiosities ... which he had made his study for five and forty years ... I found an extremely pleasant party of young people in the house which added much to the gratification & delight of the expeditions which under the Doctor's guidance we undertook ... the Dr himself was so good as to convey me back to Coleraine where I got into a post chaise ...

I must not proceed before I make some observations upon the people who inhabit this northern coast. They are principally colonists from Scotland, who migrated here in the reign of James 1st, bearing almost all the Scotch Mc attached to their names & speaking with an accent by no means indigenous. They are moreover almost all either Protestants or Presbyterians ... & in general I should say by no means disposed to grant to the Catholics the free exercise of those rights which they themselves enjoy...The lower orders seem extremely courteous, civil, and obliging, and their cottages much better than those in the country, whence they originally came. Attached to them they have also generally a few acres, which serves them with necessaries for their families ... potatoes, corn & flax. For the land they pay about £2 per acre, & for labour rarely more than a shilling per day. In these times of scarcity indeed I can not conceive with such low wages how they contrive to exist, for had it not been for the vastly plentiful supply of fish, which have been this year caught upon the coast, a famine must nearly have been the consequence ... Upon the whole tho' they appear a happy people. The city of Derry originally built by some London adventurers in ye time of

Londonderry

James I, to whom large grants, of now very valuable property, were then made, whence it has derived its name of Londonderry, is seated upon the declivity of a hill, which gradually rises from Loch Foyle ... It is surrounded by a wall which now serves its inhabitants for a promenade, and in the evening is generally enlivened by a band of the military ... I took the opportunity of visiting Loch Swilly, hiring a horse & riding down it as far as Buncrana, an expedition with which I was highly delighted ... hemmed in on every side, by vast rocky mountains ... My road laid thro' a rugged mountainous peninsula famed for its excellent whiskey and belonging entirely to Ld Donegal. Unfortunately it is let out in considerable tracts upon long leases, which are always renewed upon the payment of a fine; which tracts again are divided and subdivided into small farms varying from 4 to 10 acres & let to the poor inhabitants at rack rent. Were it not indeed for the very large illicit distillation ... it would be utterly impossible for the poor people to pay their rent ... The proportion of the Catholic population to the Protestant in this district is, I believe, almost four to one, all very peaceable, but living in a state of the most profound ignorance. It is much to be lamented indeed that some means are not taken to establish a national system of education, as it might tend to ... remove many of those prejudices, to which they are now so firmly attached. Upon leaving Derry, I found it necessary to adopt some other means for seeing the country, than travelling in Irish postchaises... as I perhaps might be inclined to visit some districts where it was impossible to obtain even these as I had a servant with me, and a good deal of luggage. I therefore determined upon purchasing a gig & horse as a conveyance and with these I very luckily met with a fair and decent price. My equipage was not indeed the most splendid, but sufficiently good for what I wanted it.

   On Tuesday Eve then I set out in quest of new adventures

Strabane

... The road to Strabane lies by the side of the river Foyle, the banks of which are all very fine & extremely well cultivated. Nothing worthy of remark except the ingenious method which necessity has taught the inhabitants to adopt of making fuel for their fire. The turf, which in many parts is so abundant, hath in this district become extremely scarce, so much so that the bog earth is the most valuable land, and in consequence, become so dear that it can scarcely be purchased by the poor people; they are therefore obliged to take a very inferior kind, which having kneaded, as it were, with their hands and feet & brought to a certain consistency they spread out upon the ground & form it into pieces the size of a brick, leaving it exposed to the sun to dry & harden.

 At Strabane, a small town belonging to the Marq. Of Abercorn I staid all night. In the morning proceeded on by Balleybofey to Donegall. The last ten miles of this road abound in all the varieties with which nature can adorn it; for nothing can be more imposingly grand, than the pass of Barnesmore or more pleasingly beautiful than the little lake of Esk, whilst the miserably wretched cabins on the former merely built with sods, without any window or chimney are a striking contrast with the neat white cottages which everywhere peep from amongst the trees on the latter. It would indeed seem, that it was the retreat of contentment and civilization, for here (the first time I regret to say since I came to Ireland), did I observe a school, which I immediately entered & commenced a conversation with the master, who really seemed a very sensible intelligent man & certainly above the situation he then held. I found that he had about 20 scholars, but that in the winter & spring quarters he had above three times the number, of all persuasions, Protestant Catholic & Presbyterian, but in the true spirit of Toleration, although himself of the Established Church, taught each his separate creed & Catechism. It is to be lamented indeed that where such men as these are found, that they have not the encouragement due to their merit, for so small was his salary, only amounting to three guineas a year & thus dependent upon the benevolence of some good country gentleman, whilst each of his scholars only pays him two shillings, & four pence per quarter, that I do not know how he could scarcely contrive to exist, & indeed poor fellow himself complained that unless the people became rather better disposed to learning than at present, that he must be under the necessity of going to some other place. Donegal ... is a small seaport, with a tolerably commodious harbour, the principal exports from which are mill stones & butter ... the situation is very picturesque & the view from it particularly fine. Hence I rode over about 7 miles to see my friend Murray, with whom I was to have come here ... He had then taken up his residence with his agent, a most respectable gentleman & quite the peacemaker of the district ... Murray was there engaged in making a survey of his property, previous to its being out of lease, in order to ascertain its actual value. His estate, which originally comprehended the two Baronies of Boylagh and Banagh granted to Ld Annandale his ancestor, in the reign of James Ist extends over a tract of country the most wild & mountainous perhaps in the North of Ireland. It commences at Loch Esk & following the line of coast from Donegal nearly to Ardara, includes a district of many hundred thousand acres, a territory equal or perhaps superior to many petty German sovereignties. And here indeed we saw the Irish in all their native wildness, many of them neither speaking nor understanding English ... After breakfast, when we had read the petitions which amounted to almost fifty every morning, we set out upon our survey followed by a suite from the immediate neighbourhood, which in the end frequently increased to some hundreds so anxious were all the tenantry to pay all due respect to their landlord & caught by the novelty of a carriage and four. At every half mile we met with what they call a town, a collection of ten or twelve cabins, inhabited by the families who have taken the farm of perhaps a hundred or 150 acres, each paying his rent according to the land he occupies. From all these issued such a swarm of men women & children, that it would have been impossible for me to have formed any adequate idea of the population of the country, had I not witnessed the fact that in some of these villages each house contained seven souls upon an average so that frequently, when in England there are three or four persons upon one farm, in Ireland there are 70 or 80. They are almost all Catholics... having never been taught to read or write ... The children, though almost in a state of nudity & filthy ... in general appeared extremely healthy & strong... The women, who are swarthy in their complexions, & harsh in their features, are principally employed in spinning the flax ... whilst the men perform the duties of the farm, which commence in March & end in October, after which time they remain in a state of the most perfect idleness, never seeking to improve their lands, or employ themselves during the whole five winter months. Some it is true employ themselves in weaving the flax, which their wives have prepared, but the generality pass their time in listless indolence ... And here it must be observed that the whole agriculture is performed by manual labour, as the spade is everywhere used instead of the plough ... So mountainous is the district, that instead of using cars, everything is carried in panniers upon the horses backs, a very tedious and laborious occupation; & I conceive by no means necessary as the roads are all good ..."

William's notice of agricultural practice and living conditions was the serious intention of his journey through Ireland. But the social aspect was beguiling—

"During one of our excursions we had the good fortune to meet with a wedding; at the celebration of which we in all due form attended, for observing a crowd of people in the open air, all dancing to the bagpipes & seemingly enjoying themselves ... we of course partook of the merriment. The general course of proceedings are these; when two young people like each other, having gone thro' all the previous ceremonies of courtship, they run off to some friend's house, where they stay some days & then declare to their parents their intention of marrying. The bargain is then to be made between the two old people, each of whom will give up something, the one part of his farm ... to the parent of the bride, as he is the person injured by the loss of his daughter's services, the other something, in general very slight, to stock it with. The bargain having at length been concluded the ceremony takes place, after which there is one continued scene of riot & revelling for three days & three nights without any interruption during which time 20 or thirty gallons of whiskey are not unfrequently drunk & of course the whole parish is in a state more easily conceived than described. It happened that it was the third day at which we attended, & therefore had an opportunity of finding the assembly in that state in which every Irishman delights, all, both men & women, in different stages of inebriation; dancing, singing, swearing, quarrelling, cudgelling & fighting, perfectly worn out & jaded & yet determined never to give up till the three days were all religiously ended ... In the parish of Kiolybegs alone, Mr Murray's agent told me that he could lay his hand upon 400 private stills in which they are not content with distilling barley but the very oatmeal for the support of their families ... We observed also that they marry extremely young as there were frequent instances in the parish, where the age of the bride did not exceed fourteen or that of her paramour 17 ... this is perhaps the groundwork of the vast increase which has taken place in the population of this country ... Having made myself tolerably familiar with the northern part of the province of Ulster I thought it necessary to continue my journey & therefore bent my course thro' Ballyshannon to Sligo. The road extends the whole way along the shore, having the lofty mountains of Benbulben &Truskmore in all their fantastic shapes towering on the left and varying every instant so that the long stages are beguiled away by the perpetual change of the most romantic scenery. I observed here also on the road side, since I entered Connaught, many stone crosses of fine workmanship, generally either near a round tower or a ruined church, which are very frequent throughout the whole island ...The country also began to assume a totally different aspect, being by no means so populous, and a much greater proportion of the land allotted to grazing, the farms being more extensive, and the cottages somewhat better. The Irish language here is universally spoken, so much so that even the people living by the road side keeping a small pot house where travellers generally bait their horses had some difficulty in expressing themselves in English. The population is principally Catholic and much more interested in their cause than any I had yet met with; this tho' may be easily accounted for ... as the gentry here are many of them of the Catholic persuasion & have called meetings in prosecution of their claims ... This I am sorry to add has been lately carried to too great a pitch as within the last fortnight ... lives were lost.

Sligo is a considerable town situated upon the water of Loch Gill, which is navigable to the town ... Hence I proceeded thro' a bleak, wild and uninteresting country to Tobercurry, where I turned out of the general route to go to Ballina, with some of the most romantic scenery in the north of Ireland. The pass through mountains rising in all their majestic grandeur from Loch Talt ... is truly imposing and awfully melancholy. Here would I

Tobercurry

recommend the misanthrope, tired and disgusted with himself & others ... to withdraw himself from the temptations of the world. Having gained the summit of the hill, the sun was just then dipping in the western ocean, illuminating with the greatest brilliancy the mountains of Donegal on the opposite side of the bay ... background to the flat country immediately below me, whilst Loch Conn with its surrounding hills were almost lost in the darkening shade ..I this day witnessed at Tobercurry ... the celebration of Mass. Having arrived about ten o'clock I observed a crowd of people collecting ... in expectation of the coming of the priest. nor were they long kept in suspense, as a poor wretched being, without shoes or stockings, habited in a rusty ragged coat which once had been black ... soon made his appearance & was greeted by the whole assembly. He was I conceive of some mendicant order ... the service commenced, when every knee was bent although in the open street & the most solemn silence prevailed ... After Mass was finished ... all the people, many of whom had come 6 or 7 miles, retired to their homes, contented with the idea that they had been purified by the holy water sprinkled upon them. At Ballina I amused myself in the evening by watching the salmon leap a ridge of rocks across the river, over which it falls forming a very pretty cascade. Here immense quantities of them are caught in baskets set for the purpose, a very valuable property for the owner although retailed out at the low price of four pence per pound. Hence I went to Castlebar across Loch Conn, a fine sheet of water studded with islands beautifully wooded ... Upon leaving this you enter a country than which it is impossible to conceive any more wild or bleak, heath rising upon heath & mountain upon mountain; a place to which Ireland might banish her criminals as Russia sends her exiles to Siberia. And yet, it is not altogether uninhabited, as here & there you meet with a few scattered cabins in the more sheltered glens ... Into one of these I entered ... I found in it three healthy little children, happy & contented ... It was built of clay, but the walls so low that it was impossible to stand upright, without any other furniture than the pan in which the potatoes are boiled, the table off which they are eaten, and the spinning wheel which supplied them with linen. At one end was the fireplace with a hole in the roof for the smoak, whilst at the other stood the cow, then being milked & their constant inmate during the whole winter. On each side lay a heap of straw, the only bed they had ... with the covering of a single rug ... Amidst this apparent poverty I nevertheless met with a reception, which would have done honour to the richest; milk, oatcake, and whatever else the best the house contained was all at my service, whilst the good woman rejected the compensation I offered, such is the hospitality which pervades the Irish peasantry."

William was now making for Westport House, the 18th century mansion of his Cambridge friend Lord Sligo. Howe Peter Browne, 2nd Marquess of Sligo, had come into his great inheritance in county Mayo, as well as a sugar plantation in Jamaica inherited from the Kelly family, at the age of twenty-one on the death of his father in 1809. Sligo was two years older than William. He was a friend also of Lord Lowther who formed part of the Regent's circle of courtiers and informants, and he had already been adventuring in the Aegean to meet Byron who accompanied him to Athens and Mycenae. He was, by all accounts, a genial, impetuous, hedonistic and affectionate young man, inclined to corpulence from an early age, without arrogance or pretention beyond the exuberant self-confidence probably natural to his rank and wealth. An adored only child, he had always a close and confident relationship with his mother, one of the three daughters and co-heiresses of the naval hero Earl Howe after whom he was named, which left him free of any but the

Westport

Westport House, the Seat of the Marquess of Sligo, from an engraving by William Daniell

mildest check on either his expenditure or his conduct. For the following year, William and Sligo were planning a continental tour together to travel southward behind the allied armies as they drove Napoleon and his forces back towards France.

"I proceeded on to Westport. This beautiful little town, which sprung up entirely under the auspices of the late Ld Sligo & which is daily improving under those of his son, is situated upon the declivity of a hill surrounded by wood ... Immediately I enquired of Ld Sligo but was told that he was then fishing in the mountains. I therefore despatched a courier informing him that I would spend a day with him ... to which I received a most hospitable answer begging me to take up my residence with him as long as I liked, & that he would be at home the following day. In order to fill up my time I went to visit the mountain of Crow

Patrick ... famous for the miracles which St Patrick there performed ... and here thousands annually visit the pillar raised at the summit to perform the penances enjoined by their priests, walking barefoot fifteen times round the station (as it is called) with blood flowing copiously from the feet of some ... Miss Edgeworth has most fully accounted for this superstitious attachment to their burying places, when she informs us that it is upon the principle of their rising together with their relations, who have been laid before them, on the great day of account ..."

Maria Edgeworth was the eldest of the 22 children of a wealthy Irish landowner in county Longford and spent most of her life in Ireland. She was a prolific novelist admired by Walter Scott and many other writers of historical novels. Her Irish novels, notably 'Castle Rackrent' and 'The Absentee' were probably her most influential.

"During all this time food is prohibited, and they are under the necessity of substituting a sufficient quantity of whiskey ...Upon my return I went to Westport House to dinner, & meeting an extremely pleasant party of old Cambridge friends, then established myself amongst them, enjoying every luxury which wealth can bestow and society and the most unbounded hospitality can give zest to."

Westport House stood on the site of the mediaeval castle of the chieftain and pirate queen Grace O'Malley from whom, through the family of Bourke, Viscounts Mayo, the Browne family was descended. The Brownes, of English origin, reached Ireland in the 16th century and proceeded as Catholics to marry into powerful Irish landowning families, gathering a considerable estate over the centuries. Westport House as it now stands, apart from some putative dungeons left from mediaeval times, is entirely the work of the Sligo family to designs by Richard

Cassels and James and Benjamin Wyatt.

"The property of Ld Sligo in this part of the County of Mayo is of enormous extent and increases daily in value as agriculture & civilization gain ground. Much indeed of the growing prosperity may be attributed to his residence at Westport and it is really impossible to form any idea, without being an eyewitness of the fact, how great are the disadvantages to the country in general of being an absentee. To understand indeed in its full force the spirit of Miss Edgeworth's last tale it is truly necessary to visit Ireland. I think no one will accuse her of exaggeration ... it does stand to reason that any one (and particularly those of such property as Ld Sligo) residing upon his own estate must be of a distinguished benefit in promoting the interest of his country as well as the happiness of individuals. There is indeed more comfort among the tenantry upon the estate at Westport, than in any other place I had yet seen ...

Having now nearly spent three weeks at Westport I began to think it was time that I should proceed upon my journey, if I intended getting round the kingdom in the course of the summer. Many inducements were indeed held out to me to prolong my visit, but as Ld Sligo was himself going to Dublin for a few days I thought it better to avail myself of the convenience of his carriage as far as Tuam whither I had sent my gig the day before to convey me forward ... Early therefore on Saturday the 28th we set out and as we had been up at a ball almost the whole night before ... I was rather inclined to sleep than to make use of my eyes ... Nor does the archiepiscopal city of Tuam hold out anything worthy of a traveller's notice, except that it abounds more in beggars than almost any other town in Ireland. Mendicity has arrived at such a pitch throughout the whole kingdom that it really has become a great burthen upon the inferior class, particularly in this year of scarcity, to supply all who ask charity even with a potato, a gift which their generosity cannot refuse ... The want of poor laws falls hardest upon those whom nature or accident has deprived of the means of supporting themselves, & thus it not unfrequently happens that the poor wretch, who is laid at one door in order to be carried upon a litter to the next remains there exposed … .as those at whose door they happen to be left are obliged sometimes to carry them two or three miles from one village to the next…"

William's diary entries are generally undated but his journey, with nearly a month spent at Westport, must have taken him well into the summer. On the 23rd June 1812 the first French troops crossed the Russian frontier, and on 24th August Napoleon ordered the advance on Moscow. The battle of Borodino was fought on the 7th September and Moscow was occupied on the 14th. Although warfare was still largely a clash of armies in open countryside and was only reported in cities, civilian travel and international trade were severely affected. Two young Englishmen of independent means planning a Grand Tour together would have to take a continental war into account. But Sligo was adventurous and William both curious and excitable. It was probably during their journey by carriage toward Dublin that plans for next year's continental expedition, to last nearly three years, took definite shape. For the present, their ways parted at Tuam.

"Here leaving Ld Sligo I came on in my gig to Galway, the country around bearing a different aspect from what I had yet seen, being principally grass or wheat land. Nevertheless its appearance is extremely cold, as scarcely a tree is anywhere visible and all the enclosures are made by high stone walls ... I discovered it was market day by the number of people ... I could not help being struck by the dress of the women which was invariably the same, being a petticoat and jerkin of coarse red

Galway

*Galway from the Claddagh
from an engraving by William Bartlett, 1854*

cloth with a blue cloak of the same material & a cap without any bonnet.

Galway is perhaps one of the oldest towns in Ireland, being originally built & colonized by the Spanish ... the streets very narrow & the houses all built of stone & have their gable ends facing the street. The church also is a very fine old gothic pile ... The next place of my destination was Gort, where I was induced to stay all night, in order that I might see the new house, which Col. Vereker is just now building ... Nothing, though, can be more beautiful than the situation. The castle, however much in general I dislike modern Gothic, is not ill suited, if he follows the innumerable examples which everywhere throughout the county of Galway obtrude themselves upon him, to grace the banks of

Dromoland

Loch Cutra. Too often, indeed, do people run into the most extreme absurdities, by building castles which they intend should represent the old baronial residences of feudal times ...

Upon leaving this I steered my course towards Kilmacduagh (that is the cell of McDuagh of the ancient family of O'Shaughnessy who here founded a monastery ... but the most singular & striking monument of antiquity here ... is a round tower of 152 feet in height, built of enormous large hewn stones ...leaning 17 feet out of the perpendicular... I should suppose intended for a belfry. Leaving this, I went on to Crusheen, and on my way paid the first turnpike since I had entered Ireland. Throughout the whole province of Connaught indeed there is not one...

Dromoland, the seat of Sir Edward O'Brien where I next went & where I was received with all that kindness & polite hospitality which to a traveller in a distant country is so extremely delightful, is another instance of the wonderful effect which a gentleman residing on his property can bring about."

It was natural that William's regard for resident Irish landowners should reach its height at Dromoland Castle and in the person of Sir Edward O'Brien, 4th baronet and member of parliament for County Clare from 1802 to 1826. He was born in 1773 and so was seventeen years William's senior. Baronetcy was the most modest rank held by the historic family of O'Brien, descended in line from Brian Boru, High King of Ireland from 1012 until 1014 when he was killed in the course of his victory over invading Norsemen from Man, Shetland and Orkney at the battle of Clontarf. They had been princes, earls and marquesses of Thomond, but accepted from Henry VIII the barony of Inchiquin. They thus became one of the very few representatives of the Gaelic nobility in the English peerage, on resigning their Irish titles, renouncing the catholic religion, and pledging

Dromoland

*Dromoland Castle
from an 18th century engraving*

allegiance to the King. Sir Edward's son Lucius duly inherited the title as 13th Baron of Inchiquin. The mediaeval Dromoland was largely rebuilt in the reign of Henry VIII, and again as a Queen Anne mansion early in the 18th century. Twenty three years after William's visit the gigantic gothic revival pile which survives was built by Sir Edward O'Brien in the last year of his life. The result might have dismayed his guest, had he seen it, but his great admiration was aroused by Sir Edward's work on his estate and the example it gave.

"Extremely fond of agriculture … Sir Edward has introduced new systems & new experiments, which have roused the interest of those around him & set a good example to the tenantry who are disposed to follow him. Exercising indeed all the virtues of a country gentleman, whose great aim is the promotion of the happiness of his neighbourhood & the furtherance of the public welfare, there is that general appearance of comfort among his dependants which I had not before witnessed in my tour. He has also established a school upon Lancaster's system, the only one which in this country from its tolerant principle can be admitted, & which succeeds beyond his most ardent expectation. Amongst the hundred boys of which it consists, there are only eight Protestants, the rest being all Catholics, with the Bible being put into their hands & the scriptures given to them in language intelligible to them ..."

The Quaker Joseph Lancaster was an educational innovator who in an age when children of poor parents usually received no education at all other than that of the Sunday school in parishes where there was one, founded the non-sectarian Royal Free School in London. By 1804 Lancaster had more than six hundred boys of the poorest parents, taught for nothing; and by 1807 there were forty-five Lancasterian schools round the country. But Lancaster was better as a prophet of education than as a

financial manager, and in 1808 he was imprisoned for debt. A committee was formed under the leadership of Henry Brougham to rescue Lancaster and the Lancasterian project, and this led to the creation of the Royal Lancasterian Institution in 1811, a year before William's Irish tour.

"Whilst I was here, I determined not to lose the opportunity of seeing all the curiosities which the county Clare contains ... My road lay thr'o a wild tract of country, which the increasing population has driven the inhabitants to cultivate, being very rugged & mountainous & which 26 years ago was intersected by no road passable by any kind of carriage. The rapid progress thro' which it has made much improvement is a subject upon which the mind delights to reflect ... ... The Cliffs of Moher, which form so magnificent a barrier against the violent inroads of the Atlantic

Moher

... rise four hundred feet in perpendicular height above the ocean. They are broken into all the rugged forms and variety of shapes, whilst at their inaccessible walls the sea dashes with such violence ... that it is frequently heard at the distance of twenty miles in the interior ...Truly may it be called an ironbound coast ... I then followed it along to Milltown and as I proceeded was very much struck by the numerous little canoes lying upon the beach, the only kind of boat which appears to be used. These are constructed merely of an osier frame covered with two hides, sown together & then pitched, of a certain length and width adapted to the waves, & rowed by two oars ... light as they appear you see them riding upon the waves with the greatest safety carried in one instant as it were to heaven & in the next buried in the deep while the fishermen sit as unconcerned in them as if sailing in the calmest sea. The Atlantic is here indeed most truly grand & in a storm sometimes so agitated that it breaks over the lighthouse on the top of Mutton island which is raised 175 feet above the level, displacing enormous rocks & carrying them from one side of the bay to the other, whilst the whole coast seems to be in a state of motion.

    The hotel at which I slept is a place of great resort in the summer for those who come for sea bathing ... nothing can be more miserably unprofitable than the way in which they seem to pass their time ... during the day quite eaten up with ennui they are obliged to recur to the dice ... or lounging about upon the beach as drag on the long hours until dinner ... Therefore I set out upon my return to Dromoland where I had been happy & where I expected to become so again. At this place indeed I think I enjoyed myself more than at any other I was at in my life. Upon looking tho' to my almanack I found the month of September was beginning to advance & I had much to see; I therefore determined to stay one day very contrary to my inclination and I

Limerick

*Limerick in 1830 by Alphonse Dousseau.
The National Library of Wales*

never left any place with greater reluctance in my life. "

The decision to move on coincided approximately with the French occupation of Moscow with all its historic consequences.

"Limerick the first place of my destination is a very considerable town situated upon the Shannon, its harbour altho' 60 miles up the river very good & commodious ... it is divided as it were, into three parts, the old town called the Irish the other the English, separated from each other by a branch of the river and built in the old stile with narrow lanes & the gable ends turned towards them, whilst the new part is laid out in very commodious streets & handsome squares. There is a cathedral of ancient date built by an O'Brien, one of the Princes of Thomond & originally Sovereigns of this & the adjoining County of Clare ... The castle & all the ancient fortifications are now in ruins, where magnificent store houses & other useful buildings are

Killarney

rising from their ashes. I dined here with Mr James O'Brien & proceeded on the next day to Listowel. The road led to the ruins of Adare a cluster of abbeys & convents ... covered in the most beautiful & picturesque manner entirely with ivy, the towers seem to rise rather out of a mass of green ... Hence I went towards the banks of the Shannon, whose course I followed as far as Glin, along a road than which nothing can be more truly grand & beautiful ... I went the next day to Tralee, a pretty little town on an arm of the sea & capital of County Kerry & afterwards proceeded on to Killarney ...fortunately it was in the close of the evening when I arrived here & had therefore no partial view of its beauties, so much do the beauties of Killarney exceed all conception ... I shall therefore content myself with giving as accurate an account as memory will allow of the few days I was here. The first day being Sunday I went to church and was glad to find in a town, the professed nursery of Catholics, so numerous and respectable a congregation ... I afterwards walked to the ruins of Muckross Abbey, situated on the banks of the lower lake in Mr Herbert's demesne... with the vast expanse of water in it front varied with the most beautiful rocky islands & surrounded by the imposing mountains of Torc on one side whilst on the other the rich places about Killarney with the Dingle mountains in the distance so grand and magnificent a scene ... in the centre of the abbey court, surrounded by a cloister, which yet remains tolerably entire, rises a yew tree, the largest I ever saw, which overshadows the whole place ... In it are the tombs of most of the principal families of the neighbourhood, and it still continues to be much sought after by the common people as the place in which they wish their mortal remains to be laid. So crowded is it that ... bones & skulls ... are piled up in heaps on every side. After surveying this I returned to Mr Herbert's to dinner and thus ended the operations of the first day. On the morrow as the morning

*The Lakes of Killarney
after an engraving by W H Bartlett, 1830*

appeared particularly clear I thought I would seize the opportunity of going to the top of McGilly Cuddy's Reeks (so called as belonging to a family of that name, originally exercising sovereign authority over the district) being the highest mountains in Ireland, about eleven hundred feet above the level of the sea. Having therefore procured a guide and hired a car I set off early & proceeded to a cabin about a mile from them where I left my horse & then commenced my march along the narrow path which winds through the glen leading immediately to their base ... a few minutes from the summit our view was intercepted by a cloud floating below us but it quickly cleared away & the scene broke upon us with redoubled splendour ... As my guide seemed a very decent & respectable man I engaged him to procure me a boat for the following day ... The next morning, therefore I went down to Ross Castle, an old building originally belonging to the family of O'Donaghue, princes of this district, but now leased out by Ld Kenmare to government for barracks, where I embarked, and steering by western point of Ross peninsula shaped my course for the middle lake thro' the channel which runs between Devil's Island and Muckross demesne ...The mountain of Glencar, at its base covered with large forest trees and above broken & rugged, masses of light & shade, & with all the varied tints of the different trees & shrubs by which it is clothed, is seen every instant in some new aspect. Passing under the bridge which connects Devil's Island & the Muckross peninsula, you enter the middle lake, much smaller than either of the other two ... It partakes indeed much of the character of Derwentwater, with bolder features & more magnificent backgrounds. Separated from the lower lake by a long narrow ridge of rocks, running out nearly two miles and broken into the most fantastic shapes and covered with ivy, yew & arbutus, it has the tremendous mountain of Torc as a boundary on the south with Glencar on the north whilst in the centre the picturesque and awful inlet to the upper lake ... still more wild and romantic than the other two, the mountains bolder, the crags more abrupt. Having dwelt upon it some time, whilst the boatmen refreshed themselves, we returned in the evening ... and relanded just at nightfall. The next day was principally employed in reviewing the demesnes of Muckross, which now bear all the marks of grounds belonging to an absentee ...The following day was spent in seeing ...the Gap of Dunloe. Setting out early in the morning we mounted our horses, and passing by one of those castles, which are scattered over these counties in every direction in vast numbers, we entered the fissure in the mountains. The road, which winds for three or four miles along a little river sometimes swelled by the mountain torrents ... which form the most beautiful & picturesque cascades,

Killarney

gradually ascends to the summit amidst enormous crags detached from the mass above and rolled down, inhabited only by the ospreys which nest in the crags, their scream the only interruption to the solemn silence ... Descending the hill on the other side, the upper lake broke upon us in all its splendour ... Thus ended the last excursion I made in the neighbourhood of Killarney, where I had been so highly favoured in the weather and every circumstance ..."

The passage that follows these fresh and impressionable descriptions shows the diarist addressing the aesthetic question of evaluating beauty in an age when romantic feeling coloured all perceptions of it, though these were still generally set in classical framing.

"It may be that I should draw some contrast between the lakes of my own country and these. I would that I found myself able in recounting the beauties of each, to devoid myself of all prejudice and view them with the eye of just discrimination. Under these circumstances I am rather inclined to think, that I must give the preference to those of Killarney, as exhibiting bolder features and more striking scenes. For the one indeed art has done much in improving those beauties which nature has bestowed, whilst in the other nothing is seen but mountains & woods, heath & arbutus all in their wildest state ... however, I do not feel myself competent to give any decided opinion ...

The town of Killarney itself is extremely good & clean all belonging to Ld Kenmare & growing rich upon the contributions it levies upon travellers. In it there is a school, preparatory to the College of Maynooth, containing about 60 boys, supported by voluntary contribution and also a small establishment of nuns of the order of St Ursula ... employing themselves in the education of the girls of the town ... The whole population of this district is catholic, being in the proportion of almost 50 to 1 of any other persuasion; but at the same time lamentably ignorant, although the County of Kerry is considered so remarkable for its learning. There are few, it is true, who are not taught to read & write as in every village there is a little school which is in general well attended, & the grain of knowledge is doled out at a very moderate price, rarely exceeding two shillings per quarter. But priests are so sedulous in not allowing the bible to be put into their hands ... that I found them reading Tom Jones or Joseph Andrews ... In some of the principal towns indeed Latin &Greek are taught, and it is not uncommon to have a petition made you for a little money to buy the "Poor Scholar", a satire, or a Greek Testament.

The language, which is here spoken by the peasantry is universally the old Irish, but greatly differing from that used in the province of Connaught. Antiquarians tho', I believe have determined, that it is by no means so pure and have pronounced it only to be a dialect or corruption of the latter. This perhaps may be accounted for by the introduction of a number of words which bear a great similarity to the Spanish, who certainly colonized many of the South western parts of the country .... This language, like all those of the East, is extremely figurative, abounding in metaphors taken from the works of nature or objects perpetually presented to the senses ..."

Following the retreat of the Russian armies after the Battle of Borodino on the 7th September, advanced units of the occupying French army reached the city gates of Moscow on the 14th. The civil governor ordered the city to be burned around the invader and fires began on the 15th, destroying three quarters of the city. French troops now embarked on a period of unrestrained looting.

Kenmore

"On Friday the 18th of September I again resumed my course ... and set out for Kenmare town ... passing through a narrow valley intersecting a beautiful range of mountains, covered with wood ... with a rapid little stream, sometimes falling over rocks & sometimes forming little lakes by the side of the road ... for 12 or 14 miles ... the bay at length breaks in on you, running up the country between two parallel ranges of mountains and varying in breadth from three to five miles. The town itself belonging to Ld Lansdowne is one of the poorest I had been in since I came to Ireland as my landlady told me it was not possible to get a pound of meat in it at that time, even if she offered for it the mines of Peru & that I must therefore content myself with the duck that was then swimming in the pond before the door for my dinner. The effects of the landed proprietor being an absentee are here —the roads neglected, the cabins going to decay & almost all the inhabitants mendicants. ...The price of labour is indeed nothing, as a man will take two hundred weight of butter hence to Cork a distance of 44 Irish miles, maintain both himself & his horse with going & returning; all for 6 shillings. Seven pence per day are the usual wages given to the labourer and a goose or turkey which almost all the poor people in this country bread may be bought for a shilling, whilst all other luxuries of this description, and especially fish, bear the same proportion. Unfortunately it now began to rain, and as I did not see any prospect of cheering up the poverty of the place it drove me out and I most rashly departed for Bantry. Nothing indeed can be conceived more truly terrific than this road, lying across a mountain which in the ascent & descent is a distance of six miles with not a single cabin near it in case of accident ... it is rarely frequented by any other means of conveyance than the panniers upon the backs of the Kerry ponies & indeed seems to have been intended solely for them. Moreover the rain continued to fall in torrents a greater part of the day ...Luckily however I got to the other side ... determining never again to undertake the Pass of the Priests Leap as it is called ... nor did Bantry upon my arrival afford me much comfort ... a dirty little inn in a still dirtier little fishing town, crowded with people drinking & smoking (it being market day) the door beset with mendicants, the landlord tipsy, the wife scolding, the children crying, the waiter stupid and the day wet did not hold out a prospect very cheering. With some difficulty therefore did I accomplish getting anything like a dinner & with still more difficulty a bed, both very indifferent and wretchedly uncomfortable. The bay, which has been rendered remarkable by the French fleet coming into it in the year 48 is one of the finest harbours in the kingdom as the whole navy of Gt Britain may ride in it at once with the greatest safety...

Next morning the road still continued bad, thro' the same bleak country, till I came to Dunmanway. And now everything seemed to assume a more favourable aspect. The people were more comfortable, the cottages better & the land more fertile. The road running all the way by the side of the Bandon river is extremely pretty and passes the demesnes of many gentlemens' places... very extensive and well wooded. The town itself seems rather neglected although it carries on a considerable manufacture of various cotton goods as well as one of linen. Hence I went to Kinsale a curious old town built upon the side of a hill, which surrounds a small bay ... Here it was that O'Connor planned the invasion of the French to take place, should they ever make a descent upon this island, and where in 1603 the Spaniards under Don Juan D'Aguilar did disembark, but being vigorously attacked by Lord Mountjoy were defeated and after an honourable capitulation were carried back to their own country by an English squadron, thus affording a precedent on the Convention of Cintra ... "

Cork

*The Cove of Cork
after an engraving by W H Bartlett, 1830*

Ceasefire agreement by British and French after Wellesley's victory at Vimeiro on 22 August 1808, whereby the French army of 26000 men, with weapons and loot, was carried home to France by the Royal Navy, provoking outrage in London.

"Cork, which was the next place of my destination is I believe the second town in Ireland, containing a population of one hundred thousand souls. It is laid out in some very handsome streets & squares of great regularity but the houses being almost all weather slated have a very cold appearance. Situated upon the river Lee, about 14 miles from the ocean, which is navigable for vessels of very considerable burden, it has every advantage for carrying on an extensive trade nor do the merchants seem at all backward in availing themselves of it ... the exports from this place consist principally in butter & provisions, great quantities of which have been shipped to Lisbon as well as having supplied almost the whole navy and fleets which collect at Cove previously to their sailing for the West Indies. The vast supplies both of meat & corn which Ireland affords to its sister kingdom is almost inconceivable, & calculating upon the returns of the Custom House of the grain exported between the 5th of January 1811 & the 5 of March 1812 it appears that she must have received a not less sum than three millions & a half of monies or of goods equivalent & that she must have had at least 250,000 acres under tillage for foreign consumption. Now considering how trifling were her exports half a century ago & also that her population has increased one fourth during that time ... upon a narrower inspection we shall find ... that this has been solely the effect of an ameliorated government, which ...emancipated her from a state of political degradation. And as such great advantages have followed the abrogation of certain laws of property, is it unfair to argue from analogy the vast benefits to be derived from dismantling those which still exist & affect the conscience? And is it not by this union that the strength of a kingdom can be preserved? ... And yet it seems to be the policy ... in the affairs of this kingdom to keep up the book of jealousy & contention instead of endeavouring to invite the two contending interests to separate them as much as possible.

From Cork I went down to Cove, going by the Black Rock to Passage, where I hired a boat which took me on. It was so late in the evening when I arrived that I could see nothing, but was highly gratified next morning by the scene which presented itself. An immense basin of water covered almost entirely with a forest of masts, surrounded by green hills beautifully fringed with wood to the beach, interspersed with a number of fine seats, gave me an idea of the riches & power of the country. I saw a number of men of war riding triumphantly protecting a fleet of merchant vessels bringing every species of luxury, which refinement can imagine or appetite can suggest. And then I could not help comparing her with the nations of the continent ... Anyone who had seen the busy bustle which I did, the number & magnitude of the vessels with their rich cargoes, would scarcely have supposed that we then had been carrying on a war for so long or that any stop had been put to our commercial relations. And yet every port on the continent from the Baltic to the Adriatic was shut against us & every people an enemy ... Nevertheless, British merchants had found outlets for our manufactures & markets for our produce.

In returning from Cove I came up the whole way in a boat, and nothing can surpass the richness and fertility of the banks all along. In the suburb of Glanmire tho' it reaches its climax; here nature & art have contrived to render it the Garden of Eden ... to the town of Cork .... The banks of the Thames at Richmond are not more polished or more improved, whilst the beauties of nature are not lost amidst the refinements of art. Having now I believe seen all that was worthy of observation at Cork I set out for Kilworth the seat of my Ld Mount Cashell, where I staid a couple of days."

The Earl of Mount Cashell's eldest son, Lord Kilworth, was a Cambridge contemporary of William. In later life he lived in Canada where he was reputed as an eccentric. He was twice married, fathered a large number of children, and died in Paddington at the age of 90.

"The country thro' which I passed, is certainly extremely well cultivated, but still wanting in wood... too often divided by stone walls or mounds of earth, hedgerows are rarely to be seen ... This part of the country has been and still continues to be much disturbed by a faction, which ranging itself under opposite leaders and separating into two parties calling themselves

Shanonites & Canaanites, is perpetually fighting whenever there is an opportunity. Unconnected entirely with any plans against the government, it arose out of a private quarrel between two individuals and has at length resolved itself into a state of actual warfare. The whole county of Tipperary has enlisted itself under these opposite banners, & scarcely a day passes, that they are not engaged in a greater or less number. But at the fairs in particular where they are collected in great bodies ... it not unfrequently happens, from the inveteracy of their hatred that two or three deluded wretches suffer martyrdom in the cause or are so disabled that they never again recover. The natural result is that it invites every turbulent spirit to join in the conflict ... Fortunately however I continued my journey without any molestation, although my servant was under such apprehension that he took care to hide his watch in case we were attacked.

On my road from Kilworth to Clonmel I met a crowd of people, attendant upon a funeral. The body was laid upon a kind of carriage under a canopy and preceded by a number of women who seemed to be in the deepest affliction ... upon enquiry I found that the most clamorous was one of those who had been hired ... This same ululation takes place also at the wake where these same women attend together with all the neighbours, who in general towards the close of .the evening turn this scene of sorrow into a feast of joy. For as the piper is always one of the party & the whiskey is most liberally distributed, dancing & drunkenness, revelry & debauchery are frequently the consequence.

The country around Clonmel is by far the most fertile and rich of any I had yet passed through. Situated in a valley, watered by the river Suir over which there is here a bridge of twenty arches, nothing can surpass the fineness of the woods or the advanced state of agriculture in the neighbourhood of the town.

Kilkenny

The Castle of Kilkenny, 1829

And indeed such it continued the greater part of the way to Kilkenny. I did not go quite so far at present as I staid & took up my abode for ten days at Desart the seat of Ld Desart."

The Earl of Desart, a cousin of Sligo, was born in 1788. He too had come into his inheritance very young, on his father's death in 1804. He was now Member of Parliament for the rotten borough of Bosinney in Cornwall.

"The situation of this house is one of the most beautiful I ever saw, commanding a fine prospect of the country below it, covered with the finest wood in Ireland overlooking the counties of Killarney & Tipperary and bounded by a high ridge of mountains in the distance. Hence I used occasionally to ride over to Kilkenny, a city whose streets are paved with marble, but not on this account the less dirty ... The cathedral dedicated to St

Canice is a heavy pile of building of the 11th century, extremely gloomy, filled with monuments of the Butler family and situated on rising ground at one extremity of the town. At the other is the castle the magnificent seat of Ld Ormond, a curious mixture of modern and ancient architecture, containing a great number of very fine portraits, principally by Van Dyke, built upon a precipice overhanging the river ... The town was completely thronged with people, who had flocked together to see or rather hear the private theatricals, which continue for three weeks with all the characters supported by gentlemen in the neighbourhood. This was unfortunately declared to be the last year of their continuance ... The party at Desart, however tho', had not the curiosity to go and witness what is so much sought after ... in truth I could never make up my mind to so great sacrifice, which perhaps says more in favour of Desart & the pleasures I there experienced than all the eulogies I could have heaped upon it - Hence I went to ... the beautiful and extensive ruins of the abbey of Jerpoint. The river Nore here becomes navigable for small vessels, as far as NewRoss. On the banks are many beautiful seats and also considerable masses of wood scattered about which adds much to the general effect ... Immediately above Enniscorthy is Vinegar Hill, a place which the scenes in the last Rebellion yet fresh in the minds of everyone cannot fail to render interesting. On the top is a small obelisk without any inscription to serve as memorial of the blood which was there spilt and which will perhaps be almost as lasting as the hill itself."

The Rebellion of 1798, following in the wake of that in America and, above all, of the early stages of the French Revolution, was brutally ended on Vinegar Hill by a British army said to have consisted of 15000 men. William's brief account, with its sober imagery, conveys some sense of the youthful Whig sympathies that were widely aroused by the first events in France.

Glendalough

Wordsworth expressed these in the famous line: 'Bliss was it in that dawn to be alive –'

" Hence I went to Arklow, a small town on the coast famous for an oyster fishery ... like every other small town in Ireland it contains a barracks for two companies of foot, and the place was then rendered very uncomfortable for me a traveller, as the inn was crowded with a regiment then upon its route. Thence the road leading to Rathdrum lies thro' the vale of Avoca, than which it is impossible to conceive anything more delightful or picturesque. This river running between two lofty banks, covered with the most beautiful and towering oaks for six miles presents at every turn some new object to admire ... No view indeed either for beauty or sublimity can exceed that which presents itself from the rising ground at the meeting of the waters (as it is called). After this the Glen presents a very different appearance. Here are some curious copper mines & a stream of very strong vitriolic water, which being received in a number of different cisterns filled with plates of iron, leaves a sediment of copper, which is of the finest quality & being collected each morning is very profitable to the proprietors. At Rathdrum a small village which is the principal emporium fighting and confusion continued during the whole night & still kept up when I left in the morning. The great reason of this conduct was, that the whole parish is divided into a number of petty factions which meet every fair day, and then try to decide which is the strongest, sometimes ending the contest in a very melancholy way. The population of the village is almost all Protestant whilst that of the neighbourhood is principally Catholic for whose convenience two chapels are built at a suitable distance. The compassionate innkeepers tho' ... having a great regard for the souls of their neighbours, each subscribe half a guinea for the payment of a priest ...thus holding out an inducement to spend the week's

Glendalough

Glendalough by William Bartlett, 1841

earnings in the alehouse and passing the Sunday in a state of riot.

Hence pursuing the same stream, whose banks I had followed from Arklow I went to Glendalough - the Glen of the two lakes- where stand the ruins of the seven churches originally founded by St Kevin in the sixth century. Situated in the wildest recess & surrounded by mountains of the bleakest aspect on the banks of two little lakes ... the seven churches are the Abbey, the Cathedral, St Kevin's Kitchen, Temple-na-Skellig, Our Lady's Church, Trinity Church & the Ivy Church. The number seven was mystical & sacred & early consecrated to religion; it began with the creation of the world and all the Jewish rites were accommodated to it. It is found also amongst the Egyptians & the Brahmins. The Irish also entertained a similar veneration for

Glendalough

*Capel Street, Dublin
by James Malton, 1790*

this number ... The Ivy Church is the first which meets the eye on entering the valley, its belfry is circular & is a first attempt towards uniting the round tower with the Church ... St Kevin's Kitchen is s stone roofed oratory, the ridge of the roof 30 feet high & at its west end is a round tower 75 feet high approximating but not completely joined to the church. Trinity Church has also part of a round tower near the cathedral which is one hundred & ten feet in height & the walls four feet thick. The ruins of these seven churches ... are now become the lurking places of foxes or the habitations of goats. Nothing indeed can give a better idea of the wildness of the place than that these very goats, which in all other parts of Ireland are domesticated and tame are here in a perfect state of nature and can only be killed by dogs or shot among the crags. In the cemetery of the cathedral are the remains of many crosses, some of very fine workmanship.

Hence I proceeded to a small lake amidst the mountains

about ten miles distant & where Mr Latouche has fitted up a shooting lodge ... I saw it ... as the evening was far advanced and the clouds lowering around it cast a deep & solemn gloom when on a sudden 'the thunder rolled and the lightning flashed' illuminating for an instant the whole scene with the most vivid glare of light. Nothing can be supposed which for sublimity could surpass the tout ensemble; the echo of the thunder among the mountains, the brilliancy of the lightning & the awful silence which ensued ... After this the evening became very dark & stormy and with some difficulty did I make out the way to Newtownmountkennedy where I was glad to lay up for the night. Immediately around this pretty little village are a great many very fine places, seats extremely convenient for those who have any connection with the city of Dublin. The country around is indeed improved in the highest degree ... Hence passing through the Glen of the Downs ... the scenery decked in all its splendour of autumnal tints... I went to Powerscourt.... having spent some hours here, I set for the great metropolis of this flourishing kingdom, only distant about 8 miles, the place which crowned the end of my tour and was my ultimate destination. To describe this city which is so well known ... I shall never attempt, feeling myself unable to do it justice. To tell the truth I felt somewhat disappointed in seeing none of the gay equipages which everywhere crowd the streets of London or the busy bustle which pervades the great commercial town. The season indeed was rather against my being gratified as almost everybody was in the country, but I believe scarcely the most ardent advocate for the Union .will deny but that the city of Dublin is very much altered with respect to its society since that event took place."

The Act of Union came into being in August 1800 and the Irish parliament sat for the last time. On 22nd January 1801 the Irish lords and commons took their seats in the first parliament

Dublin

of the United Kingdom.

"The strong proof I think was that during my stay and for two months before there had not been a single place of public amusement open; not even a theatre of the meanest description where an idle traveller could go to spend his evening. That its commerce has increased and prospered & that the merchants have risen into taking the place of her nobles & her gentry is equally certain but nevertheless the city in general I think it must be accepted wears rather the appearance of a provincial than a metropolitan town. Her public buildings indeed are most truly magnificent and upon a scale that would do honour to the capital of the most extended empire. The House of Parliament, the Custom House & the Courts of Justice are all unequalled by any public buildings which the metropolis of the sister kingdom has to boast of and are perhaps chefs d'oeuvre of the art. Great improvements are also now making by renewing many of the old streets & converting the shabby houses into handsome and commodious habitations. Upon the whole indeed I trust in time it will regain its former gaiety & splendour. Having staid here three days ... I embarked on board a collier on Thursday the 16th and after a most uncomfortable passage I arrived at Whitehaven on Saturday evening very glad to set foot again upon Old England and enjoy the comforts and blessings which she so liberally holds out to me."

On the 18th October, the day following William's landing at Whitehaven, the French army began its retreat from Moscow. When the 95000 remaining Frenchmen marched out on the 19th their retreating train was augmented, and hampered, by thousands of waggonloads of loot. William's twenty third birthday was imminent, he had been four months in Ireland and he was to set out on 13th October 1813 for a continental tour which lasted three years.

Map of Central Europe showing the principal cities visited

PART II
The Grand Tour: 1813-1815

Diary, undated
"To see the wonders of the world abroad had been my ambition. I remember the delight I had in reading books of travels, and the longing I had to follow the footsteps of the writer. My imagination was pining to see in reality what I only knew by description ... An opportunity at length offered of visiting the European continent, the channels to which had so long been closed against us by the tremendous power of our most mortal enemy. This was not to be neglected. I should have been only too happy to have gone by the frozen sea of Kamschatka, or have made the long detour of the Straits, to get a footing upon it. The tournure of political affairs was also beginning to change; all the great powers of Europe were leagued against France, and some partial successes had been obtained; the passions were then all in action, a general revolution was on the point of taking place, everything, in fact, conspired to render a tour upon the Continent at that moment peculiarly interesting, and it was impossible to resist the temptation."

With passions at work and revolution imminent, travel was hazardous. Roads were damaged by passing armies, relays of horses depended on chance, and the route was dictated by rapid military developments. But on 24th September French forces had begun to retire behind the Elbe, and William started on his journey early in October 1813 from Harwich where he and his travelling companion, Lord Sligo, were waiting to set sail for

Gothenburg in Sweden.

Since they had parted company on the road between Westport and Dublin in June 1812, Sligo had suffered a disgrace which could have seriously reduced a man less fortified by wealth and temperamental ebullience, though with the help of these he had evidently risen above it. In December 1809, aged twenty-one, he had started on a first continental visit which took him from Falmouth to Lisbon, and thence to Gibraltar where he and a college friend, Michal Bruce, were introduced to Lady Hester Stanhope setting out on her adventures. Bruce and Lady Hester soon became lovers, but she appreciated Sligo's kindness and generosity: "Where have I a relation who has been as kind to me as he has?" she later wrote. From Gibraltar they sailed in April for Sicily and then to Malta, the centre of British naval activity in the Mediterranean and hub for the distribution of post to scattered expatriates in wartime. News from the island was therefore quick to reach London.

One piece of news, soon widely known, was contained in a letter sent in May by Sligo to his mother: "I have got a most capital ship at last! She has ten eighteen pound cannonades ... 500 cartridges aboard besides canisters of grapeshot and 600 balls ... to make a defence against almost any privateer." French privateers, or licensed pirates, were particularly active and successful in the Mediterranean in attacking British trading vessels unprotected by fast sloops or small warships. The Pylades, a decommissioned naval sloop, had a crew of twenty five and was hired by Sligo for £200 a month plus wages and supplies. By order of the Admiral in command on the island, Pylades was fitted out for the grandson of Admiral Lord Howe by naval riggers and was ready to sail by the end of the month. But Sligo, wanting more trained men, sent retainers out into the bars and brothels of Valetta to recruit them. They brought back eight enlisted naval seamen in a drunken state and with these men on board the Pylades set sail for the Aegean. This dangerously rash pursuit of private adventure in time of war, with a constant need of manpower on the seas, soon roused the Admiralty in London to investigate and led to consequences which Sligo continued blithely to ignore. The Pylades was boarded and searched at sea by officers of H.M.S Active but Sligo kept the deserters well hidden. He landed first at the island of Milos where they now abandoned him before giving themselves up and returning to Malta, ready to give evidence to save themselves from the penalties for desertion. Sligo, relieved of their presence, was left to sail on to the mainland with a crew now numbering forty-five including, according to Lady Hester, "a Tartar, two superbly arrayed Albanians equipped with silver-stocked pistols and silver yataghans, a Dragoman, an artist to sketch views and costumes, a Turkish cook and three English servants, two of them in livery." But by now the legal process had begun its course and these ornamental troupers were soon forgotten.

By mid-June the Pylades was at anchor and Sligo was exploring Athens and the surrounding country, intent on excavations and discovery of relics and sometimes accompanied by Byron who was reputed to hate all antiquities. They parted company at Corinth, and Sligo rode on to the Peloppónese capital Tripolitsa where the Turkish provincial ruler, Veli Pasha, received him with feasting, entertainment, and the gift of a horse. Sligo offered the Pasha a pair of cannon from the Pylades which was accepted in exchange for "six columns of Verde antique and some other trifles," as Sligo reported to his mother on 3rd August. These marble columns, reunited with parts then missing, were later shown to have come from the Treasury of Atreus at Mycenae and were given to the British Musum by Sligo's grandson. The Museum presented replicas which adorn the south front of Westport House.

From near Corinth, Sligo re-embarked for the last time on the Pylades and sailed for Athens. In early September he finally dismissed the ship and its crew while he continued his adventure of excavating for treasures, and arranged transport to Ireland of the total haul of more than a thousand pieces. But it was not looting that concerned the Admiralty. "The Marquess of Sligo is in a great scrape about his kidnapping the seamen," Byron wrote to his friend John Cam Hobhouse. "I, who know him, do not think him so culpable as the Navy are determined to make him. He is a good man." Nonetheless, by the time of his return to London in August 1811 it was evident that the Admiralty was determined to pursue the case. "Lord Sligo has got into a very indiscreet scrape which is likely to be tried at the Old Bailey" wrote Lord Auckland, lately Chief Secretary for Ireland. The trial opened on 16th December 1812 in a packed court before Sir William Scott, younger brother of the Lord Chancellor, and presided by the Lord Chief Justice Lord Ellenborough. Sligo admitted the folly, rashness and indiscretion of his conduct but the judge ruled "that no rank, however high, no fortune, however ample, no regret, however sincere, could prevent the enforcement of justice," and Sligo was found guilty, fined £5000 and sentenced to four months' imprisonment in Newgate.

The case and the sentence naturally provoked great excitement and scandal, but the prisoner's wealth meant at least that his time in Newgate passed as comfortably as possible. His mother, meanwhile, had taken a fancy to the judge Sir William Scott which was reciprocated, and Byron informed Sligo on his release that Scott was "about to pass sentence of matrimony on his mother." The marriage was not a success, going from bad to worse until the Admiral's daughter informed the Admiralty judge

Harwich

that *"You married me, I am ashamed to say it, partly from a sexual appetite (which you should have been ashamed of yourself, at your advanced age) but principally to gratify your pride in having a Marchioness for your wife."* The marriage did not recover, but Lady Sligo had prudently put her fortune into trust beforehand, and her son developed cordial relations with his step-father and former judge, based on shared archaeological interests. His relations with his mother, as evidenced by his letters to her, were those of a libertine assuming a similar disposition in a sympathetic parent. By October 1813 Sligo had put the episode behind him, and his later career saw his reputation, never lost in Ireland, restored and growing.

William Crackanthorpe's first letter home to Newbiggin was from Harwich on October 13th 1813.

"My dear Mother,

I have this instant received Sarah's (*his younger sister's*) little note, which followed me from London down here, and has found us in the midst of a shoal of sharks, such as Custom House officers, inspectors of aliens, and a crew of I really do not know whom. The wind is now blowing most favourably, and I expect we shall sail about two o'clock, unless in the meantime an order comes down to detain the packet till to-morrow to take out a messenger. We scarcely know of whom our crew will consist, as the foreign mail coach is not arrived. There are in waiting, however, an aide-de-camp of the Prince of Orange, a Russian messenger, and some Swedish merchants. Thank heaven no ladies are yet arrived, for, however much I admire them, I cannot say that I think their company would be very desirable on board. Everything looks most propitious and seems to smile upon us, and seven or eight days will, I trust, set us down safe in Gottenburg. We have got a foreign servant along with us who speaks all the languages, and an extremely useful creature he appears to be. I shall write as soon as I get to Gottenburg, but of course when you will get it will depend very much upon the wind. It is possible we may be there in eight hours, And now I must only add, God bless you all and take you into His holy keeping is the earnest prayer of your affectionate son, Wm Crackanthorpe.

I have just seen our baggage aboard, our carriage shipped, and all the arrangements made. We have got a little cabin containing four berths to ourselves, which will make us more comfortable. There are two German officers just arrived, going out to join the Duke of Cumberland."

Sligo and Crackanthorpe were now accompanied on their journey by Count Joseph Constantine Ludolf, son of an indigent German diplomat whose last post had been as Sicilian ambassador in Constantinople. Ludolf's mother was from a dragoman family of Constantinople. Sligo had befriended the young man there and taken him back to Ireland, and thence to London, where he seems to have rapidly attached himself to Sligo's notoriously impulsive mother. She referred to him as 'my adopted son' in a will of 1814 bequeathing him a massive legacy which, on Sligo's hurried return, was reduced to a more modest immediate gift to help re-establish him in Constantinople.

The relations between the three young men during the hazards of their journey through Germany were put under strain. By the time they reached Vienna, Sligo had determined to free himself from Ludolf, though unsure how to do it. He wrote to his mother on the 4th March 1814 that "Ludolf has been so much discontented with everything all along the road and has so often expressed his regret at having ever left England that it is extremely unpleasant to travel with him. '

Gothenburg

Diary, undated:
"About midnight on the fourth day the most tremendous gale of wind came on which the captain even himself had almost ever experienced, a man who above twenty years has been accustomed to these northern seas. When I got up in the morning and went upon deck, the sea appeared to be like moving mountains covered with snow, so tremendous was the swell and so white with foam; the rain fell in torrents. We observed a small galliot, close under our bow, lying to, like ourselves, under the least possible sail, and apparently in great distress. Nothing could be more beautiful than to watch her different positions, carried at one minute as to heaven, and in the next completely hid from us by the intervening waves, but the scene was much too awful; the sea was perpetually breaking over her ... And it was utterly impossible to have rendered her the least assistance ... The next morning the scene had changed. I left my berth to find a fine, clear sky overhead, and that we had entered a most magnificent bay, surrounded by mountains of rock, without the least symptom of vegetation or a tree to be seen. As we passed along we appeared to sail through a forest of masts, more than five hundred having been collected to sail with our convoy to England, containing all the riches of the shores of the Baltic. The harbour is perhaps the finest in the world, and capable of containing many thousand ships. At this instant there are not less than two thousand lying in it, and perhaps British property to the amount of twenty millions now in the town. As we proceeded we saw many melancholy effects of the storm by which we had been visited, many vessels having lost their masts, others their anchors, and a great number on shore upon the rocks; so extensive, indeed, was the damage that we were informed that the loss of the underwriters could not be less than a million sterling. Gottenburg appears to be a very well built town, through the principal street

Gothenburg

of which runs the river; the houses are of stone, and much like English ones. Our reception has not been very hospitable; there is no room for us at either of the principal inns. We are therefore obliged to take lodgings, and dine at a table d'hôte. We have, however, beds with us which, I expect, we shall find very useful in this country."

Letter to Charlotte. October 15th. Gottenburg
"The rooms in the houses, although they imitate the English as much as possible, have by no means their comfort. What I miss most of all is the chimney piece; nothing but German stoves, and thereby not the comfort of a good fireplace; no carpets, and a most plentiful abundance of filth. I expect we shall leave on Monday for Ystadt, which is about two hundred English miles hence. I say English because seven of them make one Swedish mile. To-morrow we exhibit our letters of credit and buy a carriage for our baggage and our German servant ... He will be our avant courier, order our horses, beds, and dinners, and as he knows every Continental language, we shall never be at a loss. I think if one of you writes every week to me that will do very well. Direct them, as I told you, to Lady Sligo, as she will have frequent opportunities of sending letters by messengers ... Number your letters also as I have done, and then I shall know if I lose any."

In Spain, Wellington crossed the Bidassoa on 7th October, and the French besiegers surrendered at Pamplona on the 31st.
Letter to his mother

"October 17th. Gottenburg
We have been so occupied in preparing harness and conveyance for our luggage for the journey to Ystadt that we have scarcely had time to do more than apply to the banker (the first person

Gothenburg

Gothenburg, by Richard Lovett

sought on arrival in a foreign country!) and to pay our respects to the governor, Count Rosen, who received us most graciously, and in true style of English hospitality asked us to take "pot luck" with him the next day. We gladly accepted, and at three o'clock presented ourselves at his door. His wife unfortunately could not make her appearance. The party therefore consisted entirely of men, about sixteen in number, amongst whom was a Prince Seipia, a Polish nobleman who is on his way to England. The dinner was extremely good, and I will, if I can, enumerate it, as I know you like such intelligence. We were first conducted to a small side table, on which were laid bread, butter, and cheese, with brandy, of which most of the party partook. This is considered as a kind of stimulus to the appetite, and is common throughout all these northern regions. This ceremony being finished, we were then conducted to the dining room, where we found a dinner set out much in the English fashion — a large silver plateau in the centre with two soups at each end. Then followed roast and boiled meat, then fish, then game — woodcock and blackcock — afterwards sweetmeats of varying kinds. We had also a variety of French wines, all most excellent of their kind, and after sitting ten minutes after dinner the dinner party broke up and retired to the drawing room, where we had coffee and a glass of liqueur, which was a signal to us all to take our departure. The whole visit did not last above three hours, a time we should think very limited in England. The conversation was of course all carried on in French. The war in Germany is very popular in Sweden, as is also that in Spain. They all seem most extremely delighted with the Crown Prince" *(Jean-Baptiste-Jules Bernadotte, son of a lawyer from Pau in the Atlantic Pyrenees)* "— speak of his conduct with the greatest enthusiasm, and seem to think he has been the saviour of the country.

I went also to church the other day. The established religion is, as you know, Lutheran — the service differs little from our own. The attention of the people I was extremely struck with ... Everything, we hear, is going on most gloriously in Germany, but although we are here actually nearer the scene of action we are much more ignorant of what is really going on than in England, so fond are the people of exaggeration and making things appear better than they really are. They all lament greatly the death of poor General Moreau" *(also the son of a lawyer, military adviser to the Russian forces in Germany and mortally wounded at Dresden in August)* "— as a loss to the good cause. The character which Bernadotte gave of him to Count Rosen was particularly fine. He said of him that he had 'une douceur angélique, un coeur de lion, et le plus grand esprit militaire que existe.'. Gottenburg was originally all built of wood, but from

Gothenburg

the numerous fires ... it has been at various times almost totally consumed. Latterly, however, there has been an injunction from the Government to replace the houses so burnt down with others of brick, so that few towns can, I believe, at present boast more splendid and uniformly magnificent residences than those which the merchants of Gottenburg have by their own industry raised for themselves. There is one part which is now lying completely in ashes, a fire having consumed it within the last three weeks. It was the only remaining one of wood. Active exertions are already making to repair it ... When the town had become of such immense importance as a depôt for English merchandise—not less than to the value of ten millions sterling being at present deposited there—the inhabitants memorialised the late King and petitioned to have the walls razed and the fortifications destroyed, inasmuch as every place of strength invites an enemy to make an attack upon it, and therefore renders private property more insecure."

Some days later: "On Tuesday the 18th we prepared to proceed on our journey to Ystadt, but before I endeavour to give you any account of the country we passed through, it will be necessary to describe our travelling arrangements. The usual mode adopted in this country is to send before you a courier or as it is called a *förebud* to order horses to be in readiness upon your arrival. This man generally proceeds the day before you and you give him a paper specifying the hour you propose being at the different stations when they always take care to be provided with the horses, and whatever accommodation you may have chosen to have ordered. In order, however, that no delay might possibly take place, Count Rosen, through the influence of our Resident at Gottesburg, was so kind as to send a dragoon as our avant-courier which gave us an air of much greater consequence than we were justly entitled to, or had any reason to expect. Our travelling equipage consisted of an English barouche, and a Russian waggon (called a *britchka*) which we purchased at Gottenburg for the conveyance of our luggage which would not go on our carriage, and the servants. To the former of these we were under the necessity of having six horses, and to the latter four, a number which I should have thought there would have been a difficulty to have obtained. In this supposition, though, I fortunately found myself quite mistaken, for no sooner does the avant-courier arrive and give his orders, than the ostler of the post immediately commands the different farmers in the district to send him at the appointed time the number required. This seems strange to an English ear, but in this country the farmers, to the number of 32,000, hold under the King subject to certain rents and duties, one of which is the providing of horses for travellers on the road, and to which consequently no objection can be made. After they have sent in their horses they are obliged to wait two hours for nothing, but after that they are paid according to the time they are detained, and for each Swedish mile which they go (which is nearly equal to seven English) they receive, from the towns sixteen 'skellings,' about 6d, and from the post houses in the country only twelve, a miserable equivalent for a day's labour … It is calculated by the Swedish economists, according to Malthus, that the labour which would be saved by the abolition of this system alone would produce annually 300,000 tons of grain. For further convenience it is also necessary to purchase your own harness, as also to hire a coachman, inasmuch as it is not always safe to trust to the charioteering skill of a farmer, and particularly if you happen to have a valuable coach of your own. Having taken all of these precautions, then, viz., hired a coachman and bought harness we set out in the greatest possible style, with our six horses, the first four all abreast driven from the box and the two leaders by a postilion without any saddle …

Ystad

We were then followed by our britchka with other four horses similarly arranged, in all forming quite a magnificent procession and a most happy specimen of Swedish posting. The pride of our parade, though, was soon to be checked by the breaking down of the britchka, scarcely a hundred yards out of the town, the axle-tree unfortunately giving way, and thus depriving us of the principal part of our suite, who were obliged to return and await the necessary repairs. They, however, obtained a courier pass, which provides them immediately with horses, made all expedition after us, and by travelling all night overtook us before we set out the following morning."

Diary: Between Gottenburg and Ystadt, October 19th, 1813
"The first day's journey was about fifty miles, passing through the small towns of Königsbracken and Warberg. The road lay through a country which, though picturesque, is extremely poor and barren, winding round the bases of high rocks, sometimes bare and sometimes covered with the juniper or low brushwood. The road is one of the finest I ever travelled along, equal to any English turnpike, as well in breadth as in smoothness, and made entirely by the farmers, who hold under the Crown, this being another of the duties this tenure is subjected to. In the evening we took up our night's lodgings at a small post house, called Morness, where our accommodations were as comfortable as possible, our courier having taken care ... The following day we proceeded to Helsingbourg. During this day's route we met with every variety of scenery: nothing could be more beautiful than the road to Engelholm, indeed quite to be compared to the finest parts of Windsor Forest. We observed the most improved English agriculture introduced with the greatest success. In the estate Engeltifta, which belongs to a nobleman ... there are many acres which are rated as high as six bushels of corn of whatever kind

Ystad

it may happen to be—rye, barley, or oats,—which, according to the then price ... averaged about £1 10s sterling. The feudal system here indeed prevails in its full rigour, as the farms are all held either under the Crown, to the number of about 30,000, or under the nobility, who have about 34,000, subject to certain limitations and duties ... those owing to the nobles being the performance of so many days' labour. The rents are all paid in kind, as they originally used to be in England, and the value of an estate is always estimated and spoken of as producing such a quantity of grain, and not so much money. The peasantry too we remarked everywhere appeared to be an extremely robust and healthy race of people, enjoying much greater comforts than I had imagined had fallen to the lot of any of that rank of life, who had not the fortune to be born under a British government. They were all extremely well clothed, and living in cottages which had the air of the greatest cleanliness and comfort, generally with little gardens before them, and exhibiting a neatness which I regret to say is scarcely anywhere to be found either in Scotland or Ireland. They are also of an extremely quick and naturally intelligent disposition, whilst I believe exertions are now making to improve it by a proper education. Their general character is that of bravery and loyalty, patient in difficulties and persevering in labour, extremely desirable qualifications for the making of soldiers, of which, I believe, they are some of the best in the world.

The poor too, I believe, are tolerably well provided for by a kind of rate imposed upon the farms according to their respective value; and this view was, I think, strongly corroborated by our never having met, during the whole of our route, with petitioners for charity ... Helsingbourg is a pretty small town lying at the bottom of a hill, immediately upon the coast, and it is of some importance as a place of trade, when the two nations—Sweden

Helsingborg

and Denmark—are not at war. At present indeed, owing to the extreme narrowness of the channel and its proximity to the opposite shore its commerce is of course totally destroyed, and the harbour is filled with gun boats. It was originally fortified, but the walls have been razed, and there are now only a few batteries on the shore in case of any sudden attack.

Elsinore and the castle of Hamlet are exactly opposite. The castle stands boldly forward only to raise the curiosity of the English traveller and to excite a desire which it is now impossible to gratify."

The so-called Gunboat War between Denmark and Great Britain had continued since the British bombardment of Copenhagen in 1807, which killed 2,000 Danish citizens, destroyed the cathedral and other prominent buildings, and led to the active alliance of Denmark with France. As a consequence of the war Denmark was declared bankrupt in January 1813.

"In our imagination we endeavoured to discover the platform whereon the ghost of his departed father made his appearance to Hamlet, and with this we had to be content. The English consul most civilly waited upon us. He was originally resident at Elsinore, but when the war broke out he had to take up his residence here. On our leaving the place we proceeded by the sea coast to Lands Kronia, keeping in sight the spires of Copenhagen, which raised the same desire in our minds as at Elsinore ... Hence to Malmoe the country is a dead flat and very much resembles the counties of Norfolk and Cambridge, completely open and without any hedges or divisions. This, of course, as there is nothing to relieve the eye, makes it extremely uninteresting to the traveller. But the land is well cultivated, Scania indeed is quite the granary of Sweden, being all arable land. The peasantry assumed a different appearance in their dress than any we had before seen, owing I presume to their being

Ystad

further removed from the depôt of English merchandise, and consequently obliged to resort more to their own produce. Around Gottenburg they differ very little from those of our own country, except the women, who wear no bonnets, but always large handkerchiefs tied over their heads, whilst in the more southern province we saw nothing but fur caps and dresses made entirely of their own manufacture, as well as after their own fashion. They were universally robust and strong, nor did we observe during a journey of above 200 English miles one crippled or deformed creature. The women indeed have not much beauty to boast of, being generally round-faced, with coarse, hard features; nor are they well made, as they have short, squat figures."

Letter to Sarah, commenced on 24th October 1813 at Ystadt, finished and dispatched from Stralsund.
"We unfortunately arrived here two hours after the last packet in the harbour had departed for Stralsund, and as the wind appeared set in contrary for the arrival of another, we were under apprehensions that we should have been detained here a week. The next morning, however, at breakfast, doubting and debating what we should do, an English officer was introduced to us carrying Sir Charles Stewart's despatches to England containing the greatest possible news, an account of the victory obtained by the allies over the French at Leipzig on the 18th."

Between 16th and 19th October was fought the battle of Leipzig, a major victory for the allies of the Sixth Coalition who largely outnumbered the French army occupying Leipzig and its defences. Overall, 93000 men were killed or wounded and 30000 French soldiers captured during the retreat on the final day. 5,000 Confederation troops defected to the allies during the battle. The defeat caused the collapse of the Rhine Confederation created by Napoleon, and the end of the French dominant influence in Germany.

"The French have been defeated with the loss of 60,000 men, 30,000 prisoners, Régnier a prisoner, and Ney wounded. The allies entered Leipzig an hour after Buonaparte left, and great hopes are entertained that he may even now be taken. This great news immediately determined us to hire a vessel, and to proceed on to the theatre of events as quickly as we could ... We sent down, therefore, immediately for the English Consul to procure for us, if possible, a ship which would convey us to Stralsund, in which having succeeded we set about taking the carriage to pieces and getting the luggage on board, and about eleven o'clock embarked with a fine wind for the 0destined port. Most fortunate, indeed, it was that the wind was with us, for the vessel had by no means a sufficient quantity of ballast to have borne up had the wind been contrary, and we must have gone before it in whatever direction it had blown. Nor were our accomodations such as to make us wish for a long passage, the cabin being so small that it could scarcely contain the Captain himself, consequently there was no place for us but the hold. We, however, made the best of it by opening out our own beds (the filth of a berth on board a Swedish vessel is more easily imagined than described) and wrapping ourselves up as warm as we could. The crew, too, were so weak and apparently so inexperienced , that I do not believe they could possibly have managed the vessel in a gale of wind, it being cutter rigged, and therefore requiring so many more hands to work it. We were very much indebted to a young Swedish officer of the navy, who had in the morning brought over Captain James in his own armed lugger, for the assistance he rendered us in lending his men to prepare our vessel for sea, as also for his convoy, inasmuch as this part of the Baltic is very

Stralsund

Stralsund from Willkomm's 'Baltic and North Sea', 1850

much infested by Danish privateers, which issue out of the island of Bornholm whenever a favourable opportunity for a predatory enterprise occurs. At six o'clock in the morning we had the good fortune to make the land of Rugen, and following the course which our Commodore pointed out to us the spires of Stralsund soon came in view, and having taken a pilot on board we were landed there after a most rapid and prosperous voyage of only twelve hours.

The hotel at which we are does not inspire us with any great idea of German comfort—large rooms without any carpets, stoves without fires, and most abundantly dirty, I can assure you. I have though, I really think, almost learnt to enjoy filth more than cleanliness, so much have I been accustomed to it since I left England. On our arrival here we were last night most kindly invited by General Gibbs, the English Commanding Officer in this town, which is garrisoned entirely with our troops, to a ball, but unfortunately our cloaths were not landed, and so we were not able to equip ourselves for it. I hope he may ask us to dinner to-day. We are going to call upon him and intend to fish for it. I am glad to say that we have again got in a civilised country with respect to currency, which is all in gold and silver; the former, indeed, was never known so plentiful as it is at present, whereas in Sweden I never saw a single coin of the country, except a few farthings, there being no silver or gold, and money being entirely in notes as low as threepence each. I trust we shall be able to proceed on our way to Berlin tomorrow. I fear we may be delayed a day, as Sligo must call upon the Duke of Cumberland, who is at Strelitz."

Sligo's grandfather, Lord Howe, was a confidant of George III and his grandmother had been lady-in-waiting to Queen Caroline. Sligo had thus been brought up in an incidental relationship with the royal family.

"(*The Duke's*) character has not at all improved by his transportation, as we hear him everywhere spoken of much in the same style as in England. He was indeed obliged to leave headquarters, as he felt that so little attention was paid to him. And now I must conclude. God bless you all; with much love,— Your affectionate brother, Wm. Crackanthorpe."

Diary: Stralsund and Berlin, undated.
"Stralsund was originally a place of considerable strength and strongly fortified. When the French got possession of it in 1807 all the works were razed, and it was left a completely open town, so that when, in the beginning of this year, they made an advance towards it, there were no means of protection for the poor inhabitants. It was, however, garrisoned by English troops, and through their exertions such works were thrown up as would, for

some time, have stopped the advance of the enemy. In these operations every one volunteered his assistance, and neither rank nor sex was exempt from having their share of the labour. Their exertions had, indeed, somewhat slackened as the immediate alarm had subsided, but we saw ourselves numbers of women using the mattock and spade with the greatest industry, and men of considerable rank submitting to the same with the utmost cheerfulness. And here we first began to perceive that this war was no longer a political struggle for conquest and aggrandisement but a most glorious contest for emancipation from tyranny and oppression. The torch we found was lighted ... the universal cry was "Down with the French," and the enthusiasm manifested everywhere was delightful. Some of the churches here are now used as a depôt for stores for the cavalry. The French converted them to this use, they are thus considered polluted by the inhabitants and have never since been put to any other. Several small chapels are also employed for the same purposes, as the immense quantity of stores which have been sent from England, of every description, for the use of the armies, almost exceed the possibility of belief. All the troops, Swedish as well as Prussian, which we saw were clothed with English manufactures and most of them armed with English musquets. Stralsund is the grand depôt where they are first landed, to be afterwards distributed, it being the only port yet open in the Baltic for British shipping.

There being nothing in the town so remarkable as to detain us we set out, after we had supplied ourselves with money, for Berlin. We hoped to have reached Teptow, a small town, in the evening, but the extreme badness of the roads in Pomerania, together with the poorness of the horses, induced us to take up our abode at a farmhouse, where, having made a statement of our case, we were most hospitably received and set down to an excellent supper of milk and potatoes with our host and hostess. Their delight when we informed them, as well as our broken German would permit, of the discomfiture of the French before Leipzig knew no bounds. They had suffered considerably from the corps under Davoust upon its retreat from Russia, as also during the campaign of 1807. Buonaparte's principle of making war support war had been fully put in force, by which the poor inhabitants of the country were deprived of everything they possessed, and were subjected to all the ravages and rapacity of a soldiery always too ready to indulge the licentiousness of their passions, without any means whatever of redress. The next night we slept at Brandenburgh, a considerable town in the territory of the Duke of Mecklenburg Strelitz, where we saw the first symptoms of war. A German legion was forming for the service of the Emperor Alexander. Here were collected soldiers of all nations from the Don to the Atlantic, there being a number of Cossacks and other Russian soldiers from their different provinces, as also thousands of deserters from Buonaparte's army of the States of the Confederation, each in his separate uniform, and altogether forming the most motley group which it is possible to conceive. Desertion, indeed, we soon saw must have thinned his ranks considerably, for along the whole road as we proceeded we found parties succeeding each other, who had come over, and immediately volunteered into the Allied service. These were quickly either drafted into other regiments or formed into separate corps, and were then immediately dispatched to the army under Walmoden.

 Mecklenburg Strelitz, whence came our Queen, is one of those small sovereign principalities which abound in Germany. Its annual revenue does not, I believe, exceed three hundred thousand rix dollars. |It was one of those states which Buonaparte forced into the Confederation, and furnished a contingent of four

Berlin

hundred men. The soil is sandy, and, therefore, poor, and the country flat. It abounds with forests of pine, which grow to an immense height. We passed on our journey through many miles of these uninteresting woods, and, with the sandy roads, nothing can be more 'ennuyant' to the traveller than the whole appearance of the country. The reigning Duke keeps his court principally at New Strelitz. He seems to have a palace in almost every town of his dominions ... and generally most miserably out of repair. He appears to be much loved by his people. Nothing indeed can exceed their ardour in the good cause, all the country is in arms, and new levies of the *Landwehr* are marched off daily to the armies, whilst the different towns are all guarded by the burghers, equipped in uniforms, and doing all the duties of regular soldiers.

The country to Berlin bears the same uninteresting aspect, without any variation whatever. It was nearly dark when we arrived at the capital, and we were therefore compelled to restrain our anxiety till the following morning, and content ourselves with enjoying the luxuries of a most excellent hotel and a much needed repose!

Letter to his mother

"Berlin, November 1, 1813

My dear Mother,—We are arrived, I am happy to inform you, safely at Berlin, after a most prosperous journey. The roads indeed in Swedish Pomerania are more miserable than any I have ever travelled over, for without any exaggeration they are worse than that from Newbiggin over the Moor to Long Marton in the winter, and had we not had one of the strongest carriages in the world we must most certainly have broken down. At Strelitz we expected to have stayed a day, thinking that the duke of Cumberland was there. He, however, had joined Walmoden's army the day before, and we therefore proceeded without seeing

Berlin

Berlin, 1814

the Court of his Serene Highness the Duke of Mecklenburg, whose whole revenue as a sovereign Prince does not amount, I believe, to £600,000 per annum, out of which he has two regiments to support and all the expenses of a Government, such as it is, to supply.

We are at present lodged in the Hotel de la Russie, under the same roof with the French General Bertrand, who is a prisoner on his road to Frankfort on the Oder. He is one of Buonaparte's best Engineer officers, and will be a very great loss to his service". *(Bertrand was a friend and companion of Napoleon and remained with him in his exile on Elba, and later at St. Helena.)*

"There are also in the Palace, prisoners, The King, Queen, and Princess of Saxony; they are under a guard but what will become of them is not known. The morning after the grand battle

Berlin

of the 18th, Buonaparte came into their room at Leipzig and begged that they would felicitate him upon the victory he had gained, but added they must be prepared to follow his fortunes and remove to his rear. They, however, said they had followed so long without any visible advantage to themselves or their country that they must decline, and should the town be taken by storm they would throw themselves upon the mercy of the Allies; upon which he got into the most tremendous rage, and after storming for some time he turned round to the queen, and said: 'Quant à votre frère il est un grand Coquin' (meaning the King of Bavaria) and so left them all to their fate."

King Maximilian Joseph, of the ancient Wittelsbach family, abandoned Napoleon shortly before the battle of Leipzig and after the Congress of Vienna his country became the largest separating Prussia and the Habsburg Empire.

"They surrendered themselves to the King of Prussia, and have been here ever since. They are treated with the greatest tenderness and humanity, being permitted to have all their attendants around them, and to go out wherever and whenever they like. We frequently see the King taking his morning drive in a coach drawn by six horses, which is not at all better than a hackney one in London, and followed by another with four, which carries his suite.

Nothing can be more magnificent than this town—the buildings most superb and the palaces beyond description splendid. It is at present however most horribly stupid, as there is no Court, and the nobles are with the army. The new streets are almost entirely composed of palaces, built with a regularity which is almost inconceivable, each one surrounded with a Grecian border en bas relief which gives them a most finished appearance. The Unter den Linden Strasse cannot be equalled by

Berlin

any street in any city for its length, breadth, and palaces. At one time it terminated by a gate after the model of the Propylaeum at Athens. The French, tho', when they paid Berlin a visit in the year 1809 robbed it of one of its greatest ornaments by sending to Paris the magnificent bronze chariot and horses by which it was surmounted.

The equipages in Berlin are most truly wretched being generally of the fashion which existed in England at least a century ago, rough and unfinished, and the harness not unfrequently of ropes, with the coachman sitting upon the near wheel horse driving two leaders only by guidance of his whip. But little advance in the art of coachbuilding has been made in Berlin, and they have no idea of neatness or cleanliness in the arrangement of an equipage. The King passed through here on Thursday on his road from Breslau. I would indeed that I had arrived in Berlin a few days earlier, that I might have seen his reception at the Opera House, coming as he did straight from the battlefield. The universal joy and delight ... which everywhere manifested themselves were altogether so overpowering that there was nowhere a dry eye to be found ... What moment would compare to this for the King! It is true that by his conduct during the whole of these difficult times he has justly deserved his people's love and confidence."

In fact King Frederick William III, having sent an army in aid of Napoleon's Russian campaign in 1812, only declared war on his French ally on 13th March 1813. The Prussian army that took part in the victory at Leipzig was commanded by General von Blücher, who still led the Prussians at Waterloo two years later. William was evidently carried on the wave of Prussian nationalistic fervour aroused in victory after humiliation.

"All the towns are guarded by volunteers, and the

Berlin

detestation in which the French are held is most universal. The militia of the country have done prodigies of valour, and, in fact, the whole contest has been carried on by the Prussians. Their army at present is estimated at 250,000 men, and it is utterly impossible to withstand ... All Germany is in arms, and really fighting for independence and emancipation. The number of deserters from the French, such as Westphalians, Dutchmen, etc., is enormous. We see them coming in every day, as also great quantities of prisoners, all extremely young, and miserably wretched looking creatures. But what is most atrocious are the waggon loads of wounded which daily pass the windows.

The English Minister not being here, we shall stay little longer I presume than merely to see the town and its environs. We shall proceed on to Vienna, where we expect to find some society. Ludolf's sister is married to the Russian Ambassador there, and we are told it is one of the pleasantest houses in the town. There I believe we may bring to an anchor for the winter. At present there is only one theatre in the town. It begins at six and ends at nine. The performance is unfortunately in German and so it is not very amusing to us who do not well understand the language. Indeed I am afraid that I shall make very little progress in it, as French is universally spoken and is the language of every Court in Europe, so that the inducement is almost done away with.

We have not found so many English travellers as I expected, now that the Continent is open again. I suppose they are waiting for the chance of entering by Hamburg, which I conceive must soon be open, for the Crown Prince of Sweden is gone to Cassel, which is in the rear of the army of Davoust, and there will be no possibility of escape for him. Indeed he is one of the greatest rascals in the French service and I trust most heartily he will fall into Bernadotte's hands, for Bernadotte hates him so mightily that he said to Count Rosen of him, 'Si je l'attrape il est un si grand Coquin que je lui couperai les oreilles.'"

Bernadotte, one of Napoleon's royal creations and ancestor of the only such dynasty to survive into the twentieth century, abandoned France for his adopted country which he led into alliance with Russia in 1812. Commanding the Swedish force he arrived late at the battle of Leipzig. He became King Charles XIV in 1818.

"I will write to you again before I leave Berlin My best love to all, and may God bless and keep you is the earnest prayer of your ever affectionate son, Wm. Crackanthorpe.

I wish you would be so good as to enclose a two guinea note directed to Miss McIntosh at Mr. Lamond's, Charlotte Square, Edinburgh, which is the half-yearly allowance my servant makes to his father, and which I have arranged to pay regularly for him out of his wages."

Diary, undated. Berlin.

"The square in which stands the theatre should not be passed over as it presents a coup d'oeil almost unrivalled. The interior, however, by no means corresponds with the external appearance; the decorations are very poor and mean, and like all the places of entertainment I have yet seen on the continent, extremely ill lighted and dirty. The orchestra is admirable. The Germans, indeed, are remarkable for their love of music as well for extreme proficiency of execution.

But Berlin is not interesting to the traveller at this moment for the magnificence of its buildings, or the splendour of its palaces; these are all lost in viewing the spirit of the people in the good cause, in seeing those bursts of patriotism and thirst after independence … The moment that I entered Prussia I saw that the war was national and not political, and that the people had taken up arms in their own defence, and that they fought under the same legend as in the year 1673, 'Pour le Prince et pour la Patrie nous sacrifions notre vie.'"

The reference is presumably to the Franco-Dutch war in which Prussia was an ally of the Dutch Republic. Of more general interest is the insight into the distinction between a political and a national war, a relatively fresh development.

"Who, at the beginning of this year, could have believed that (Prussia) would have had two hundred and fifty thousand men in arms to have opposed to a power under whose yoke she had so long groaned? But, happily for the world... there was enough energy to engage in another struggle upon the result of which depended their very existence. To do this the greatest sacrifices were called for, all luxuries were to be given up, and every species of private convenience, for the public good. And what a glorious example did the women of Berlin set to the world in general. Not merely content with giving up their jewels and ornaments of value ... they universally and with one consent carried to the treasury their very wedding rings. In return for these they received one of iron, with this motto inscribed: 'I receive iron in exchange for gold!'

Hospitals, too, have been established in different parts for the sick and wounded, and for the use of these, women, even of the highest rank, employ themselves entirely in making bandages and preparing lint, whilst many whose fortunes would permit it have undertaken the care of a certain number of wounded in their own houses.

With such brilliant examples of devotion in the one sex, the other could not be backward in doing its duty, consequently not less than 150,000 men were enrolled, disciplined, and equipped in less than six months ...Nothing could resist the tremendous shock of their first outset, and particularly of the new troops, who were always the foremost to expose themselves. The battle of Internock, indeed, was perhaps one of the most brilliant affairs; this victory was gained by the *Landwehr*, the impetuosity, and, at the same time, the steadiness of whose attack the French were utterly incapable of withstanding. The towns, too, are all guarded by the shopkeepers, who, neglecting their own private affairs, have volunteered to perform all the duties of the garrison… whilst the reserves are all ready and anxious to come forward whenever the moment shall arrive. Whenever you turn your eyes you meet but one spirit and hear but one voice, which calls aloud for the independence of Europe and the deliverance from French oppression.

In the neighbourhood, about a mile out of the town, is to be seen one of the most interesting houses which the King of Prussia possesses. It is at this villa of Charlottenburgh where he passes most of his time, and where the late Queen is buried. She lies in a beautiful marble temple, built in the Doric style. Nothing can be more melancholy than the whole appearance of the place."

Queen Louise, who died in 1810, was known as an energetic and dominant woman, more popular than the King, and a champion of Prussian nationalism and territorial expansion. At Tilsit in 1806, after Napoleon's defeat of the Coalition, she attempted unsuccessfully to cajole him into granting Prussia merciful peace terms. The terms were punitive and deprived Prussia of all possessions west of the river Elbe, as well as of Prussian controlled parts of Poland.

"Leaving Berlin we passed through Potsdam, which was the favourite residence of the great Frederick. It was here, indeed, where many of those Machiavellian schemes, which were the foundation of so much misery to the world in general, were

Leipzig

planned, and for the adoption of which perhaps it has been the fate of the kingdom to endure so many hardships. There is one room in the place which one almost shudders to enter. It was the place where those deeds of darkness must have had their origin, where, for fear, as it were, of the light shining upon them, Frederick and Voltaire used to shut themselves up. It is a small library, scarcely large enough to contain more than themselves and the table over which these political and atheistical principles were hatched. It had a communication with the kitchen below, and thus they were supplied with all the food they wanted without the interruption or intrusion of a servant. Nevertheless, one cannot see the place without thinking of the genius of Frederick the Great, and almost admiring his policy. This feeling soon passes, as one remembers that he was ... the cause of the general bouleversement of the world, moral as well as political ..."

Letter to Charlotte.

"Leipzig, November 12TH, 1813.

My dear Charlotte, I have forgotten to whom I wrote last, whether to you or Sarah; but as I conceive a letter from me will not be unacceptable, I have given you the right of primogeniture. Our departure from Berlin was rather hurried. The road all the way to Leipzig is what is called a *chaussée,* that is, paved with stone, and each side planted with a row of poplars which are so very formal that if it passed through a picturesque country the view would be completely spoiled. But nothing is spoiled, as the country is extremely monotonous. On our route we met perpetual convoys of French prisoners, going to Russia who had been taken at the late battle of Leipzig, all in a state which would have excited the compassion of the most unfeeling. Starved as well with hunger as with cold, almost naked, exhausted with fatigue and distress, we saw these miserable wretches driven on with an

Leipzig

Declaration of Victory after the Battle of Leipzig, 1813, by Johann Peter Krafft

inhumanity which nothing but the most dreadful exasperation against everything French could possibly have induced. Scarcely able to crawl along from exhaustion and fatigue, compelled to march on at the pleasure of their guard (the peasantry), and when actually sinking by the road most unmercifully beaten to force them to rise. In one instance, indeed, of the most uncalled-for cruelty, we ventured to remonstrate, but we drew ourselves into danger without effecting any good — for, surrounded by half a dozen gensd'armes, we were threatened with a coup de sabre, and had we not been well armed I really believe we should at least have undergone the same punishment from which we wished to rescue these more unfortunate Frenchmen. The prisoners all appeared extremely young, few above 21 years, and

Leipzig

totally unfit to bear the fatigues of a campaign. But what will be their state before they shall have arrived at their destination? All are to go into Russia, some possibly to the deserts of Siberia. If such was the fate of those we met they must perish, and I can only say, may God in his mercy make them partakers of a happier world. Following the great road from Dassau to Leipzig we easily traced all along the different bivouacs which the French corps under Marshal Ney had taken up in its retreat, and as we approached nearer the town more evident signs of war shewed themselves in the straggling carcases of dead horses on all sides.

But with what feelings did we enter Leipzig, only a short fortnight ago the scene of such horrible carnage? To every Englishman, of course, to tread the ground upon which the independence of Europe had been regained was to cause a feeling of exultation, but, when we saw the misery which was the consequence, I can assure you the sentiment seemed completely to vanish. On every side we saw broken carriages, dismounted guns, carcases of horses, articles of clothing of every description, immense tumuli containing thousands of brave souls, and not unfrequently bodies which had been overlooked, lying in a state of putrefaction. The inhabitants were employed fifteen days in burying the dead. The carnage, indeed, was most horrible. Scarcely less than 80,000 souls must have perished between the 16th, the day the fight began and the 19th when the Allies took possession of the town. The battle of Borodino, a wounded French officer has since told me, was not to be compared with it, either for vivacity of the fire or the impetuosity of the troops. Death or victory were the only feelings that governed the troops; and happy were those who died on the field of battle in the performance of their duty, for their sufferings were but momentary compared to what the survivors have undergone.

In the hospitals were found 23,000 French soldiers, beside

Leipzig

the wounded of the allies. Every church is filled with wounded; not one is left vacant in which service can be held. Crowded together, too scantily supplied not only with medicines and attendance, but even wanting the very necessaries of life, it is not to be wondered at that the most horrible fevers have been engendered, and that the mortality in these receptacles of misery have been almost inconceivable, not fewer sometimes than 900 or 1,000 dying in one night. Twelve wagons were continuously employed in carrying the corpses to the grave ... the ghastly visages of the dead shamefully exposed to view ...

The streets, too, are crowded with poor miserable wretches, who have lost an arm or a leg. I fear that but little attention is paid to the feeding of them, as you see them picking up the very refuse at the door ... In consequence of the horrible devastations of the country round, there has not been a sufficiency of provisions, and many therefore have died of want alone. The season, too, has been against the recovery of the sick, for the weather is more like April than November.

What does the greatest honour to the victorious troops is, that although the town was taken by assault, yet nevertheless it has not been at all pillaged, and but for the miserable human objects creeping about the streets, you would never discover that it had been the scene of so terrible an engagement. The *faux bourgs,* of course where the battle waged hottest have had some homes battered down, the gardens by which Leipzig is surrounded are a complete waste, having been occupied by the troops, as places of bivouac — the trees cut down for fire, and the shrubs used by the soldiers for covering in the sheds as some sort of protection against the cold of the night, but otherwise the people are now all employed as usual in their common occupations.

This is indeed the most complete discomfiture Buonaparte

Leipzig

has ever suffered, having lost in one day 140 pieces of cannon (which I myself have counted this morning), and at least 60,000 men, he having sacrificed three whole divisions of his army, as also the influence over the whole of the German States which form the Confederation of the Rhine. It may be expected, perhaps, that I should give some actual account of the battle. To do this, though, I feel utterly incapable, as I am unacquainted with the different portions of the corps d'armée. All I know is that the town was attacked successfully at three gates, that Buonaparte retired by the fourth and soon afterwards blew up the bridge, by doing which he sacrificed three divisions of his army, in order, I presume, to save the rest. During the 18th he was mounted upon the *potence* (a place where malefactors are executed outside the town) making his plans. When in this situation, it is said that his guards jokingly exclaimed that he was 'dans sa propre place'. He did not leave the town till half-past ten on the morning of the 19th, and before he left making the visit I told you of in my last letter to the King and Queen of Saxony, saying, 'Il faut que vous me félicitiez sur mon grand succès car j'ai gagné une grande bataille!' The gate by which he intended to have gone out was so filled with cannon and baggage that he could not pass. He was therefore obliged to go through a garden over a temporary bridge made on purpose for him. He slept that night at a village not above an English mile distant from the town, and there collected the remains of his shattered army.

What the actual loss of the French was it is difficult to ascertain. There are 18,000 prisoners, besides 23,000 sick and wounded found in the town, and perhaps 20,000 left on the field, while the allies will not have fewer than 30,000 men placed hors de combat — and thus we have nearly 100,000 of our fellow creatures either deprived of existence, or of the means of enjoying it, merely to gratify the inordinate ambition of one man.

Leipzig

We have found a very pleasant family in that of the Governor of the town, a Prince Resnia, a Russian. We have dined there two or three times and also passed the evening. His wife, indeed, is a most charming woman, with a great deal of 'esprit', and whose manners and conversation are extremely prepossessing. The society at the house is principally military. I there met General Jomini, whose conduct has been so much canvassed, and whose book upon tactics has gained him so much credit. What his real merits as a soldier are it is not for me to decide, for I am not sufficiently acquainted with the motive that led him to quit the French. As an acquaintance I can certainly say that I think I have scarcely ever found any one with whom I was more amused, or who had greater powers of conversation."

Jomini was a Swiss born soldier who served in the Peninsular War under Marshall Ney, and again under Ney in the campaign of 1813, before defecting to the allies on August 15th. He had been sent by Napoleon on diplomatic missions to St. Petersburg and formed a close relationship with Tsar Alexander, which prompted him to refuse a command in the Russian campaign.

"Having heard here of the different positions of the armies, and that the headquarters of the Emperor were removed to Frankfort, we shall, I think, set out thither tomorrow morning as we should like to see the allied army if possible, and stay a few days at headquarters with Lord Cathcart and Sir Charles Stewart. You will in future however, I hope, hear regularly from me. I must now conclude with best love to my mother and Sarah, and may God bless you all.

Your affectionate brother Wm. Crackanthorpe."

Diary. Leipzig to Frankfort
"The first night we slept at Weimar, the capital of that small principality. The palace is extremely handsome, and much larger

than any we can boast of. On our way we passed over the plains of Lützen. With what feelings must Buonaparte have looked upon that ground where, only a few months since, he had hoped to have subjected the whole world to himself, and to have dictated peace on his own terms, not hastening away as a fugitive, with only the shattered remains of his victorious legions, uncertain where to make a stand. Well might he have wished that he might have died like Gustavus, the place of whose fall is marked by a small stone on the roadside, and thus have been saved from the sea of troubles now overwhelming him. Happy for all had this been so; the lives of thousands would have been spared, and that accumulation of horrors which we afterwards saw would never have taken place.

We were obliged to avoid the town of Erfurt, as it still had a French garrison. We had, therefore, to make a circuit, and as the roads were so miserable that we were stuck fast for some hours in the mud, uncertain whether we should not have the happiness of spending the night in the carriage. Moreover, there was a possibility that if the enemy had chosen to make a sortie in that direction we might have been surprised, as we were within half a mile only of the town; we should then have had the satisfaction of being locked up in the Citadel as prisoners of war. At length, by repeated exertions, we managed to proceed, and by putting into requisition all the horses in the neighbouring village — at one time we had no fewer than fourteen —we contrived to arrive at Gotha about midnight. Our German servant, indeed, contributed much to our advancement by the dreadful lies which he invented to impose upon the country people, calling us Princes and Generals (and I know not what other titles), who were bound to be at headquarters by a certain time!

And here, again, how bitter must have been Buonaparte's reflections as he passed through the city where, only a short time ago, that conference of crowned heads had been held. At that time, by the success of his arms, he had gained an influence which swayed the whole Continent, and totally destroyed the equilibrium of power. At present he was flying through with a most disastrous precipitation, and not without the danger of his being taken prisoner by the Cossacks who formed his avant garde.

Thuringia, through which we were now passing, is a beautiful country. Instead of the flat monotonous surface, hills covered with woods arise on all sides. At the little town of Gismach we were told we were the first English travellers they had seen for seven years, and the postmaster testified his joy by treating us with the best his house could afford, and refusing any compensation. The French, indeed, in their retreat had not left much behind. They pillaged everything they could lay hands on, and further wantonly destroyed what was of no use to them. They were here pressed very hard by Blücher's army, and gained some slight advantage. And here again the actual horrors of war presented themselves. On each side of the road lay bodies of men and carcases of horses yet unburied. We passed whole villages burned so that not a single shed remained for the miserable inhabitants. Every town was pillaged of everything useful and valuable. Who, then, with such a picture before his eyes, would not execrate the name of that being who, for the gratification of his own ambition, has not only turned this smiling country into a desert, but murdered its inhabitants and destroyed their homes?

At Hanau we were again on the battlefield. Here the misfortunes of Buonaparte seem to have risen to their culminating point. The inhabitants were all employed in burying the dead, and as we passed along many were the brave souls we saw thrown into their graves without a tear shed over them, or a prayer uttered for their blessing. The indifference with which one

Hanau

*The Battle of Hanau, 1813, by Horace Vernet.
National Gallery, London*

at last, by habit, looks upon these fallen trunks, is truly astonishing; and, however unfeeling it may appear, I must declare I felt great interest in viewing the different expressions on their countenances. Upon some there was a settled calm and tranquillity, such as only the consciousness of duty in death could have produced; in others I remarked a ferocity which told of the spirit animating them, whilst to others the agonies which they had endured were but too plainly marked. My mind was filled with awe and melancholy ...

Of the warmth of the contest the town bore strong marks. Many houses were laid in ashes, and others perforated in a thousand places by the fire of cannonry and muskets. It was taken and retaken three times in one day. The Bavarians nobly distinguished themselves. Although opposed by a force superior in numbers and commanded by the first Captain of the age, they made a resistance which has not been surpassed ..."

The balance of manpower at the battle of Hanau, fought on October 13 was approximately two to one. Napoleon's remaining force was of 100,000 survivors, against a Bavarian army of 43,000 men under General Wrede who lost 9,000 of them in the fighting. 70,000 French troops were able to reach Frankfort on 2nd November, leaving 100,000 now isolated in Germany as the retreat continued towards the Rhine. All surrendered in the following weeks bringing total French losses during the Allies' campaign for Germany to roughly 400,000 men.

Letter to his Mother.

"Frankfort, Dec. 13th, 1813

My dear Mother, — As the Emperors, Kings, and other great personages have not yet left this place, we of course could not think of separating from such good company, and have therefore prolonged our stay. We now understand that there is a probability of their moving on Tuesday, in which case we shall set out on Saturday so as not to be delayed by want of horses on the road. 'On dit' that the reason for this place having been headquarters for so long is that there is some kind of negotiations going on, which some hoped might end in peace. Of the nature of these negotiations we, however, know nothing, diplomatists being ever surrounded by an atmosphere which it is impossible to penetrate. Certain it is that offers of some kind have been made, and that couriers have passed between the French and the allied powers. I believe it is now known that these efforts have not been successful, and that active operations will soon recommence. The troops are already in position on the banks of the Rhine. One immense corps has defiled into Switzerland (to be called the 'Grand Army'); another, under Blücher, is near Coblenz; and a third is ready to co-operate with the Dutch. The greatest unison

Frankfurt

Frankfurt, 1840

prevails, and all looks well, but though, as an Englishman, I cannot help rejoicing in the downfall of the French, I must regret that the overtures for peace have failed. No one but those who are eye witnesses can possibly have any idea of the miseries of war. Famine and pestilence almost invariably follow, and the thousands who perish through hunger and fatigue, even in the best organised armies, are almost inconceivable. Then there is the devastation of the countries passed through, and the excesses which the soldiery, the Cossacks particularly, are guilty of. The inhabitants of such a country are truly wretched and miserable. Buonaparte is concentrating his force at Metz, a very strong city, having withdrawn all troops from Mayence. It is said to be the intention of the allies to besiege Metz.

Frankfurt

I must give you an account of how we pass the day, and then you will be able to judge whether it is not almost time that we should be tired of it. We breakfast about nine, and very soon afterwards have a levée of those people who choose to come and see us; then we go to the Casino (or in vulgar language, the Coffee Room) and read the newspapers. Afterwards I am generally lucky enough to find someone to lend me a horse to ride for an hour; and at two come home to dinner, which we generally take either with Lord Aberdeen or Sir Charles Stewart. At six the Play commences, but as I very soon get tired of that amusement, I generally come home. At nine a Madme. Bethmann, who is ready to receive anyone after their first introduction, is always at home. There you meet all the great people, and I am so much accustomed to see Princes and Grand Dukes, and entertain so humble an opinion of them — almost all — that I am quite afraid of becoming too democratic!"

The Bethmann family were owners of a banking business rivalled only by the Rothschilds. They were Protestants and continued to occupy powerful positions in Germany into the twentieth century, under the name von Bethmann Hollweg..

"Thus pass our days, one very like another, and, but that we expected that something interesting would have resulted from the negotiations (probably a congress opened) we should, I think, have taken our departure long before this. I have seen English newspapers up to the 9th by the messenger who arrived last night. I expect that letters will not be longer than ten days in going to Vienna.

The county I see has been vacant by the death of Lord Muncaster, and by a letter which Sligo has had I understand Lord Lowther has been canvassing it with great success. I beg, therefore, that you will not fail to give me an account of the election, and particularly of the speeches, as I am sure they

Frankfurt

cannot fail to be amusing.

    This town does not contain much of interest. It was formerly a free town, but since the revolution it has been granted to the Grand Duke, who was one of Buonaparte's great favourites. He has, upon this sudden change, abdicated in favour of Beauharnais, and has retired to the Sea of Constance to avoid falling into the hands of the allies. The merchants are immensely wealthy, and their houses are palaces by no means unworthy of the Emperors and kings who at this moment inhabit them. Great quantities of wine of the better kind are made from the vineyards in the neighbourhood. You may have it at from 2s to 7s a bottle. I would, indeed, that I could send some home, as it would be a very pleasant summer drink.

December 14th.

    I have just had a conference with Sir Robert Wilson. He tells me there will certainly be no armistice. There are at this moment 700,000 troops stationed in different situations by the allied powers against France, and all ready to carry on the war at once. We shall, therefore, start for Stutgard tomorrow, for, as we shall be on the line of communications between the different armies, we shall only get forward very slowly. I am afraid, too, that as we no longer have the opportunity of sending letters by messengers, you may be even longer in receiving them than hitherto. My best remembrances to all who may enquire for me. My best love to Charlotte and Sarah. God bless you all. — Your affectionate son,

                      Wm. Crackanthorpe."

Diary.

"Frankfort could not fail to be interesting, being the temporary abiding-place of so many crowned heads, and still more so of that group of men to whom the affairs of Europe are at this eventful time entrusted. For there are at this moment within its gates two Emperors, two Kings, and I know not how many sovereign princes, with their different suites, civil as well as military. To be indeed in the midst of these heroes, who have by their valour accomplished such unlooked-for results — the transferring of the war from the banks of the Moskva to those of the Rhine, the leading of the warriors of the Don and the hordes of Tartary to meet their foe in Germany — is a cause of gratitude. But apart from these circumstances, there is little to detain the traveller in this city. In the Cathedral the Emperors of Germany, as long as such a title existed, used to be crowned …

I must not forget to mention the outposts at the little excursion we made to Hochheim, where is the bridge over which Buonaparte passed when crossing the Rhine. Hochheim is about 16 English miles distant. It is famous for its wine, and is situated upon a hill completely covered with vineyards, which were occupied at the time of our visit by about 10,000 Russian troops en bivouac, who had greatly destroyed the vines. Below lay the town of Mayence, strongly fortified, and presenting an extremely imposing appearance. In the background, stretched the hills of France, whilst to the north and south the eye wandered up and down a country unparalleled perhaps in richness and fertility, a country soon to be the scene of war, to be robbed and exhausted, its happy and contented peasantry soon to be made wretched and miserable …

The Russian advance posts to which we descended were within half pistol shot of the French vedettes, and no sooner had one left them than we heard some coups de fusil which passed between them in a little affair caused by the indiscretion of someone who had passed the line prescribed. But there is at this moment so good an understanding that you may often see the French and Russian soldiers drinking their brandy together.

Frankfurt

A remarkable circumstance occurred in the gallant affair which ensued when the allied army took possession of Hochheim. After an obstinate resistance of some time, they were at length successful, and took the town by assault, and the French were expelled from it with the greatest precipitation. Whilst pursuing them on the other side, at the *pas de charge,* on a sudden the view of the Rhine broke upon the troops when, electrified as it were by the sight, they, by one impulse, made a halt, and for a few minutes an absolute, almost awful, silence prevailed. Then, with a tremendous cheer they renewed the pursuit with double ardour, and caused the French to pass the bridge at Mayence in such confusion that the scene upon the Bergen can only be considered inferior to it both in its horrors and its after effects. Thousands of poor creatures hoping to save themselves if they only gained the opposite bank, crowded upon each other with such violence that they were either crushed to death by the cannon and baggage then passing over, or trampled under foot by the cavalry; others finding it impossible to make their way threw themselves into the river, and trusting to their swimming powers, which in many cases proved insufficient, perished in the water ... And thus ended that memorable retreat, which has been marked with horrors too shocking to humanity to think of, in which Buonaparte certainly lost not fewer than one hundred and thirty thousand men by sword, famine, and fatigue, forfeiting for ever his reputation as a soldier, breaking the charm of his supposed invincibility, and transferring the war from the banks of the Elbe to his own territory on those of the Rhine.

It is curious to think that scarcely ten days ago Frankfort was as much an integral part of France as Paris itself! Never again, I trust, will Buonaparte be able to have Germany in subjection, and the Confederation of the Rhine ... must now be dissolved. The different Princes of which it is composed have every one of them

Frankfurt

come over to the cause of the allies, and have volunteered to double the contingent which they before furnished. It is Prussia in particular which has been the grand instrument by which the expulsion of the French has been effected ...

The allies are evidently determined not to allow Buonaparte much repose. The campaign will be continued through the winter, and it is very well known that the French are arming rapidly. For myself I shall be sorry to see the integral part of France invaded, and I trust Holland and Italy may be rather the principal objects of attack. What one must, most of all, wish for is peace. A friend of mine, whom I have found here, an aide de camp of Sir Robert Wilson, had the good fortune, in the battle of Leipzig, to take possession of the carriage of Buonaparte's Commissary General, in which he found the returns. Buonaparte's forces then amounted to nearly 230,000, and it has been pretty well ascertained that not more than 80,000 followed him to Mayence ... As yet we have none of us received any letters at all, nor do I expect that we shall till we arrive at Vienna. I shall not be sorry for a little rest. My head has begun to be in such a state of confusion that I cannot arrange my ideas, or do anything with earnestness ...

We have met with very few English travellers, considering that the Continent is now open. At many places we were the first they had seen for years past, and glad they were to receive us. At the same time, though, I believe it is more for the love of our coffee and sugar, than for any respect they have for ourselves; for much as we do and have done for them, I fear they are not altogether so grateful as they ought to be. In Prussia, indeed, it is perhaps just at present otherwise, but in general we are not liked. At a general peace they say the power of England must be crushed, as well as that of France!

And here for the moment ends the memorable campaign in which we volunteered our services, though as lookers on only,

Frankfurt

not as soldiers. It being the first time we have followed the tract of war, we feel inclined to make a vow that it shall be the last, so great an impression have the horrible sights we have seen made upon our minds."

Frankfurt to Stutgard
"... We slept the second night at Heidelberg, a little town on the river Necker, situated in a most romantic valley. The ruins of the ancient castle, the ancestral home of the Electors Palatine, stand boldly above the town. At present the castle is completely in ruins, having suffered as much from the war of the elements as from mortals. It has been twice struck by lightning, as well as besieged several times during the 30 years' war ... By a singular coincidence, two places (Bittenfeld and Lützen) have been twice chosen as battle ground — the same stretch of country has been run over and has suffered all the horrors of war which two hundred years ago was its fate. But how different the objects of the two wars! In the one the contest was for the establishment of ... tolerance of opinion, in the other for existence as an independent political body — in fact, the one for spiritual and the other for temporal ascendancy."

The battle of Lützen was an inconclusive but certain French victory fought on 2nd May 1813, at the cost of 20,000 lives on each side. Napoleon and Blücher commanded the opposing armies until Blücher was wounded.

"I must not forget to mention the great tun which stands in the Castle of Heidelberg, containing 200,000 bottles of wine, and which used formerly to be tapped annually upon the birthday of the Grand Duke of Baden. It has not now, though, been filled for the last forty years, and is completely fallen into decay and is unfit for use ..."

Letter to Charlotte.
"Stutgard, Dec.12, 1813.
My dearest Charlotte, — According to the plan which I mentioned to my mother in my last letter, we left Frankfort on the 6th, and after a most delightful journey of three days arrived here. We drove through a most beautiful country, winding round the bases of hills covered at the top with pine woods, frequently crowned with the ruins of baronial castles, whilst the lower slopes are converted into vineyards. Very different was the landscape to any we had met with in North Germany, where are nothing but pine forests and sand plains.

With all this smiling fertility, the people are by no means happy, being oppressed by the rigours of an arbitrary Government, and threatened by war. Tyranny is carried to its greatest height in this kingdom of Würrttemberg. The most arbitrary measures are executed. No one dare make the least resistance ...For instance, the King is extremely fond of shooting, and in order that he may gratify his passion for sport, the ancient game laws are in full force. By them, any unfortunate peasant who may happen to kill a stag or roebuck eating his corn is punished with death. As a consequence, game has increased to so enormous a degree that the whole country is devoured by it, and during the summer, for two or three months in succession, all the inhabitants are obliged to watch their crops by day and by night ... Again, no officer dare appear out of uniform, under pain of being sent to a fortress for two years, an offence which with us is punished at most by his being put under arrest for a couple of days.

The debts of the Crown, too, are most enormous. Nothing is paid for, and all finance is in the most ruinous state. It is impossible to imagine anything more wretched than the state of the whole country. France itself has not suffered more from the

Stuttgart

oppression of Buonaparte than this little kingdom of Würrtemberg under the absolute and despotic sway of its newly made King. That he is unpopular cannot be wondered at. I believe nothing is more ardently wished for than the accession of his son to the throne. But not a murmur of discontent dare be uttered; everyone trembles, and the system of espionage is, I believe, perfect, as it is founded on that best of all models — France.

I must now endeavour to give you some description of our reception at Court. As Englishmen we felt it necessary to pay our respects to the Queen, and therefore immediately on our arrival we sent our cards to the Great Chamberlain, saying that we wished to be presented in order that we might do so."

The Queen of Württemberg was the eldest daughter of George III; until her marriage, Princess Royal. She died in 1828.

"Our message was quite à propos, for Prince Henry of Prussia, with some Russian generals in charge of a considerable corps d'armèe, happening to be making a short stay here, it was thought necessary to entertain him by giving some kind of a fête every evening, and by chance this evening a ball was the amusement fixed on. An answer was thereupon immediately returned, commanding our presence, and ordering us to be at the palace at half-past six for a previous presentation to the King, the Queen being so unwell that she could not see us. I wish I could convey to you any idea of the splendour and magnificence with which this Court of Stutgard is kept up. Upon our entrance into the hall, which was filled with a body of men clothed in the ancient Brabantese costume (corresponding, I believe, with our Yeomen of the Guard), we mounted the grand staircase, and were ushered into a saloon lined entirely with the different marbles of the country. We then passed through a suite of apartments, each one more richly decorated and furnished than the other, and at length reached a room where the King, surrounded by his family,

Stuttgart

received us. Having asked a few questions and conversed a while most graciously with each of us, he went out into a gallery filled with the company invited to the ball, when, having quickly paid his respects to them, he made up his party at whist, and retired to another room. We then joined the general company and began to dance, keeping it up till nine, when supper was announced. The dances were generally English country dances, with an occasional waltz and a French cotillion, as it is called. About 250 sat down in the grand saloon to a most sumptuous repast. The covers were all of plate, and there were not less than 150 footmen, in state liveries, beside *jägers*, pages, chasseurs, and all the rest of the ridiculous figures which were ever heard of in any Court. After supper, dancing was again resumed, and kept up with a great deal of spirit till midnight, a most rational hour for sober people to go to bed, and, unfortunately, just about the time when these revelries begin in London.

 The palace is the most superb building; not fewer than fifty rooms were thrown open this night, and all en suite, all lighted up with crystal lustres. The King's apartments alone are twenty eight in number, and these are prepared for him every night exactly in the same way as on the most State occasions. The Queen unfortunately did not appear. She suffers from some complaint which forbids her to dress herself. She was good enough to express to us, through her daughter-in-law, the Princess Royal, how happy she was to hear of the arrival of her countrymen in Stutgard but, having recently refused to see the French ministers and other people on the score of her health, she must decline seeing us. I am afraid, poor woman, she suffers much. She is maltreated by the King, and except for once or twice in the year is never seen by anyone in or out of the palace, except her own immediate attendants. Circumstances, too, have rendered her lot more miserable than it might otherwise have been. She has been denied all communication with her own family and country for ten years. She has seen the French dictating what terms they pleased to the whole of continental Europe. She has been obliged to receive Buonaparte in person, and has witnessed the misery caused to the people of her husband's country by tyranny and oppression. Her private charities in the town are unbounded, and she is beloved by all.

The Princess Royal, the daughter of the King of Bavaria, and whose husband will succeed to that throne on the death of his father, is a most charming woman. We were introduced to her, and each of us had a long conversation with her upon different subjects. Sligo indeed danced with her, and tomorrow I believe we shall go to her house to a private party. We were also presented to the Grand Duchess of Oldenburg, sister of the Emperor of Russia, who happened to be passing through on her way to Schaffhausen. A more attractive woman I think I never saw, and from the questions which she put to more than an hundred persons presented to her, addressing each in his proper language, I should say remarkably clever".

Ekaterina of Russia was a granddaughter of Catherine the Great. A famous beauty, she was much loved by her brother Tsar Alexander I who wrote to her "I am yours, heart and soul, for life ... to love you more than I do is impossible." Napoleon, at the suggestion of Talleyrand, considered marrying her as his second wife; her family promptly arranged a marriage to the Grand Duke of Oldenburg. She died in 1819 at the age of forty.

"Stutgard we have found extremely pleasant and agreeable. We are the first English travellers who have appeared here for years, and so delighted were some of the people to see us that I really thought they would have embraced us publicly in the streets, such an effect did our red uniforms produce. The Court

Stuttgart

*The Market Square in Stuttgart
by H Schonfeld*

here exceeds in splendour that of any other in Europe — our own cannot be compared to it, either for the magnitude of the establishment or the regular state which is kept up. And every other thing corresponds, the carriages, horses, and above all, the household troops, who for the richness of their uniforms and the fineness of their men, exceed one's utmost imagination. With all this parade, in which his Majesty of Württemberg delights, he is by no means happy. Ever afraid of coming to an untimely end, the Palace is surrounded by a numerous guard, whom he takes very good care to keep in his interest by paying them most regularly. Unfortunately they are the only people he does pay. The poor tradesmen who furnished the Palace in this most magnificent style have not yet received one sou of payment. It is the same with all the other purveyors. They are left completely without remedy or redress.

Stuttgart

The universal estimation in which Lord Wellington is held as a General throughout the whole continent is most flattering. He is openly called the 'First Captain of the age,' having done more with less means than any other man in the world could have done. And I am extremely happy to see by the *Frankfort Gazette,* which is this instant arrived, and which, being published in French, is the only newspaper I can read, that he has again gained considerable advantages and added laurels to his crown. I am afraid I can send you but little public news, in fact no one knows anything; the whole occupation of the officials seems to consist in the arrangements of etiquettes and Court ceremonies, varied by parades of the troops stationed in the town. These are all new levies, and, wonderful to say, it is the third army which has been formed during the last three years. The first was totally destroyed in Russia — only three hundred cavalry and about as many infantry being left out of twelve thousand. The second was destroyed in Prussia since the opening of this campaign, and the third, which numbers 25,000 men, has just marched to the banks of the Rhine to try (I hope) its better fortune. Everything looks well. Hemmed in on every side, with the horrors of war transferred to his own country, Napoleon must, I think, at length sue for peace, and set the world at rest. But do not think the contest over! It will yet be a severe one, and France will not succumb without making desperate efforts.

We shall, I think, stay here some days longer. We have found a very pleasant society in some Hanoverians, attached to the Queen, who, of course, are only too happy to throw their houses open to any Englishmen. There is also an English family who have been resident here for a very great many years. They have almost forgotten the language! The Comte, indeed, is Grand Chamberlain to the King, and we always therefore apply to him to instruct us in all the forms of etiquette, which I can assure you are most strictly observed — affairs which I find very tiresome, and in which I am very little versed.

We shall then, when we are tired, make a little detour by Schaffhausen to see the falls of the Rhine, and the Lake of Constance, and thence on to Munich where Ludolf has an aunt and some other relations. We shall stay there two or three days and then proceed straight to Vienna. This letter goes by a special messenger, who has been sent here for the Queen's despatches for her family. I fear we may hardly meet with another before we get to Vienna. Do not, *therefore, be surprised or alarmed if it should be some little time before you* again hear from me. With best love and an earnest prayer that God may bless you all, believe me, your affectionate brother, William Crackanthorpe.

P.S. — It may be interesting to the Temple Sowerby politicians to know that a very poor opinion begins to be entertained of the Crown Prince of Sweden, and that he has lost his character very much, as well as a military man as a well-wisher to the good cause."

Bernadotte, a Frenchman by origin, was reproached with arriving late at the battle of Leipzig, and afterwards with concentrating his attention more on Swedish territorial ambitions than on supporting the allied armies. Sweden acquired Norway from the Danes by the Treaty of Kiel in 1814.

Diary

Stuttgard.

"... With a small principality which scarcely exceeds in its revenue the income of some private individuals in England or that of many of her rich nobles, Württemburg boasts a list of offices in the Court Calendar as numerous as those of the Red Book, and a palace which in extent exceeds any which the sovereign of Great Britain possesses. Each of the reception rooms are hung and furnished with a different silk or velvet, each contains a picture, a statue, or a vase which have been brought from all parts of the world, at an immense cost, to gratify the taste of the king. Nor is one only struck by the splendour and richness of the surroundings, so happy are all the arrangements that the palace has completely the air of comfort of the house of any private individual. Nor is it only inside the palace that this magnificence is displayed, but it is to be found throughout the whole of the Royal establishment. The stables cannot certainly contain fewer than three hundred horses, all in prime condition, whilst the number of carriages of various descriptions (many of them built and finished in a style which would do credit to the best English manufacturers) is prodigious. The Court is kept up in a blaze of brilliancy, such as no other in Europe can boast of, with a household much more exhaustive than that of the King of England, chamberlains and maréchaux, jägers and maîtres de cérémonie abound. They are obliged to be in attendance every day. The daily ceremonial gives one the idea of the magnificence of an Asiatic Prince rather than the Court of a small European sovereign. These officers of state are compelled when on duty to wear uniforms, all more or less superb and gold embroidered, decked, too, with 'orders' and 'grandes croix.' A simple individual is apt, 'au premier coup d'oeil,' either to feel himself humble amongst so many glorious beings, or, reasoning too much in the abstract, to hold at nought these supposed honours, gained perhaps at the price of meanness and servility. The effect, however, I must confess, is extremely imposing.

    The form of government established here is that of the most absolute monarchy, all authority resting with the king, without any control whatever. Everything being thus at his disposal, the lives, liberty, and property of his subjects at his caprice. Lettres de cachet are freely issued, by which an unfortunate individual is shut up in a fortress, no reason being assigned for his imprisonment, and no opportunity being given him for proving his innocence.

I fear that the King of Württemberg does not use his vast power and opportunities well. Blest with talents which, rightly used, must have made him conspicuous among the German Princes, he now exercises the sway of a tyrant that is hated by all, and but one prayer is offered — for his speedy removal. His whole Court, indeed, visibly trembles when he makes his appearance, and even the members of his own family are silent in his presence.

His treatment of the Queen is quite unworthy of a man. Shut up in her own apartments she is allowed to see no one but her immediate attendants; she participates in none of the pleasures or gaieties of the Court, and is compelled to find amusement in her own resources. Being entirely obedient to the will of her husband, she is never allowed to exercise her own judgement. For years she has been denied all communication with her own family, by which cruelty she could not fail to be deeply affected. She is beloved and pitied by all ranks, and with justice."

King Frederick died in 1816 and was succeeded by his more liberal son, King William I, who gave Württemberg its first parliamentary constitution in 1819. Queen Charlotte outlived her husband by twelve years.

"The contingent which Württemberg furnished as a member of the Confederation of the Rhine was 12,000 men. These were raised by a conscription exactly as in France. The conscription exists here in all its rigour still. No rank is exempt from its honours, and no substitution is permitted, so that at this moment many men of family are in the ranks and sharing the lot of common soldiers. A more complete body of men than the Gardes du Corps I never beheld. Any sovereign in Europe might be proud

Stuttgart

of them, particularly the squadron of Cuirassiers, who have a yellow uniform with a cuirass and helmet, the last of the most classical shape, of polished steel. The officers have their cuirasses and helmets of silver, and the effect of the whole is really splendid."

The Württemberg contingent, later calculated at 14,000, was almost entirely wiped out during Napoleon's 1912 Russian campaign. What William saw was therefore a decorative remnant displayed by an unpopular tyranny.

"The population of the country does not amount to more than 150,000, and these principally profess the Lutheran religion. Absolute tolerance to all other religions is however allowed. The revenues of the Crown are estimated at about 15,000,000 francs. The great exertions which the state has had to make in the raising and equipping of so many troops for the late campaigns had increased the burden of taxation fearfully. The inhabitants are now paying nearly a third of their actual income in taxes. Duties have been put on various articles of consumption, but in general the taxes are direct. In spite of his love of splendour, show, and magnificence the King is a great economist. He administers the whole of his establishment himself, and inspects most closely all the expenditure of the State.

A singular coincidence occurred one day whilst we were at dinner. An Austrian officer sent up to us, saying that as he understood we were English travellers he should be very happy to present himself as a compatriot. Of course we desired him to come up immediately, and had a cover laid for him to make up our party. He called himself Aylmer, told us that he had been in the service since the year 1798, that he had never since that returned to his native country, which we discovered to be Ireland, asked many questions about his family, and in fact spent the whole evening with us chattering on many subjects. Upon his taking leave, however, which was very late, he came into Sligo's and my room, took us by the hand and said, 'I will not deceive you, I hate the idea of it, my name is Aylmer. I am one of the rebel generals, who after capitulating was obliged to leave the country.' He then entered into the whole details of the circumstances in which he had been engaged, recapitulated the whole history of the rebellion, and told us all the particulars of his adventures, and then left us, having raised in us a very considerable interest in his favour, an admiration of his frankness, and a hearty desire and wish for his future welfare. It was impossible for anyone to be more penitent than he was, more anxious for the good of his country, or more sincerely sorry for the part which he himself had so unadvisedly taken."

William Aylmer led the Kildare rebel army which survived for months in 1798 in their stronghold as the Irish attempt at revolution failed. They received no reinforcement, no instructions from the organizers of the revolt in Dublin, and no help from France, backer of the attempted revolution. Aylmer tried to negotiate terms of surrender as the Wicklow and Wexford armies continued the fighting until the end of July when they too surrendered. An amnesty followed and Aylmer with other leaders was sent to Dublin where they were held in the Royal Exchange, but eventually permitted to go into exile.

Aylmer returned to Ireland after the Napoleonic wars and rejoined the army. In 1819 he sailed to Venezuela in command of the 10th Lancers to support Simon Bolivar's independence struggle. He died of wounds in Jamaica in 1820

On December 22nd 1813 the first allied troops crossed the Rhine to commence the invasion of France.

Diary. Stutgard to Vienna.
"We left Stutgard on the morning of the 3rd January, accompanied by Ludolf's brother, a young officer in the Austrian army, who had leave of absence for a few days, which he spent with us. He was then returning to his regiment.

The first night, in consequence of the badness of the roads, we had the pleasure of spending in the carriage, as we did not reach the place of our destination till four o'clock in the morning. The circumstances too were not agreeable; the rain was falling in torrents, the night was excessively dark, and we were in a country where every village was occupied by the corps d'armée which we had seen pass through Stutgard previously. Amongst them were between five and six thousand Cossacks. These gentlemen do not always make a just distinction between *meum* and *tuum,* and we were therefore not without apprehension lest they should take it into their heads to stop and plunder us, for they consider everyone who is not a Russian their enemy, and also they have a right to appropriate whatever they meet with in a foreign country.

The different bivouacs through which we passed were extremely interesting, as they gave one a view of another side of the miseries of a campaign. The soldiers, however, although the cold ground was their bed and the heavens their only covering, did not appear unhappy. On all sides we heard the sentries chanting one of their national airs, ands groups of men sitting round the fires they had lighted, apparently contented … We passed through Hechniger, the ancient capital of the small principality of Hohenzollern, whence came the reigning house of Prussia. It is one of the most ancient titles in Germany, and from time immemorial the Hohenzollerns have exercised the rights of sovereignty. It now contributes a contingent of 97 men to the allied army. It is the smallest principality in Germany, measuring some six square miles, with a population of 10,000 souls. The Hohenzollerns were at first only Counts of the Empire, but in 1653 they were made Princes, and were given, in common with all the other sovereigns of Germany, the right of life or death over their subjects, that of making war, of concluding alliances, and of having their own coinage. At first sight this appears quite ridiculous, for many of the German sovereigns, of which Hohenzollern is the feeblest, can scarcely furnish fifty soldiers, still it may be these gradations of power are as necessary to the wellbeing of the great political machine of Germany as are the gradations of light and heat for the natural world ...

We crossed the Danube, which is here quite a small stream at Tulthoven, and here entered on a country which is called the Schwarzen Wald or Black Forest, so named from the gloomy effect of its vast pine woods. It is inhabited by a race of men whose character differs wholly from that of the other people of Germany. Living secluded from the world, they have preserved many of the customs as prescribed by Tacitus. They speak a peculiar *patois* and have a unique costume. That of the women is very striking. It consists of a small gold or silver embroidered cap, placed at the very back of the head, from which hang two long cues of plaited hair. Round their body they have a stuff jerkin, and upon their breasts they wear an embroidered cuirass, wrought in various colours. The richer have them of the precious metals. Round their waists they appear to wear a rouleau, which, with their very short petticoats, detracts much from the elegance of their figures, and, with their bright red stockings, gives them a very grotesque appearance. This people live in small wood cabins remotely situated in the forest, and they get their living by cutting the wood and preparing it for exportation. They are very clever in making small toys, and their dolls are noted throughout Germany. From living so apart from the world they

Schaffhausen

The Rhine Falls at Schaffhausen by Birket Foster, 1878

still retain more of their original character, and their manners are at once more chaste and more simple.

During our stay at Schaffhausen we visited of course the famous falls of the Rhine, which are within two miles of the town. This is indeed a most noble scene, where one of the finest rivers of Europe is precipitated over rocks of at least 100 feet in height. The foam which rises from it forms a cloud which can be seen at two miles distance. We arrived at Schaffhausen at the moment two Austrian corps d'armée entered the town, thereby breaking the neutrality which the Swiss desired to have maintained. Once indeed I thought they might have made some resistance, as all the gates were barricaded, and the windows filled with soldiers, waiting only for the signal to fire when the Austrian troops should make their appearance, but, frightened by the numbers, and understanding what must be the consequences, they very quietly retired and allowed the Austrians to cross the Rhine without opposition, the Swiss troops, on their side, crossing the river to the canton of St. Gall. This act was certainly a most positive violation of public law. The Helvetic body were assured by a convention of 200 years' standing binding them to furnish a quota of 16,000 men to France, and, I believe, that by the public law and established usage of Europe it is no act of hostility to supply such a quota under such a treaty. As to the neutrality of Switzerland being disadvantageous to the allies, that does not alter the question of the *laws of nations*. Another time the neutrality might be equally disadvantageous to France. The impression created by this act was distinctly unfavourable, for, to begin with, violating the neutrality of Switzerland was hardly the best way of restoring the independence of Europe. It is difficult to come at any exact knowledge of the sentiments of the Swiss people. I believe, though, that the canton of Schaffhausen is by means favourable to the allies. A dread of Austrian dominion obtains, and with the memory of the battles of Sempach and Mongarten fresh in the mind of every independent Swiss, this cannot be wondered at. The Austrian troops, however, behaved admirably. They passed through the town without offering any violence to the persons or properties of the inhabitants.

Constance contains nothing of interest. It gives its name to the most rich and powerful Bishoprics of Germany, at present in the possession of Dahlburg, the Grand Duke of Frankfort, the man to whose advice Buonaparte owes the scheme of the 'Confederation of the Rhine.' "

Archbishop von Dalberg looked to Napoleon to create a unified Germany and was made Prince-Primate of the Confederation of the Rhine. His attempts to federalize the

Munich

component states failed and he went into exile in Zurich late in 1813.

"In this part of the world the houses are all built of wood, and as a protection against fire the figure of St. Florian with a bucket of water in his hand is painted upon them as a safeguard. In all Catholic countries each town and each district has its particular patron saint, whose image is stuck up in every corner — an object of adoration to the vulgar and of faith to the believing."

Letter to his Mother

"Vienna, Jan. 10th, 1814.

My Dear Mother. — As we only arrived here last night and I have only this instant heard of an English gentleman's departure for England I must not lose the opportunity of sending you a letter, though you must excuse me if I defer giving so circumstantial an account as I could have wished of all we have seen and heard since we left Stutgard.

Munich is by far the pleasantest place I have yet been at on the Continent. Nothing could exceed the kindness shewn us by all ranks of people, from the king to the peasant. The society is upon a more pleasant scale than any I ever in my life saw. Upon our arrival we announced ourselves to the Grand Chamberlain as wishing to pay our respects at Court. Upon this the Prince Royal sent for us to command us to attend his levée in the evening. He kept us chattering and talking with him for a couple of hours. He speaks English with tolerable fluency.

The way in which he abused Buonaparte was quite delightful, calling him a 'hateful little Corsican rascal,' 'an abominable liar,' 'a man with whom he hoped the allies would never make peace,' and in fact in all respects speaking the sentiments of a true Englishman. A delay arose about our

Munich

Munich from a steel engraving, 1836

presentation to the King, as no English Minister has yet arrived, it was therefore three days before we were asked to a Court ball when nothing could be more gracious than were both the King and the Queen. The following day we were asked to dinner by the King himself, who came up to us and said 'You'll dine with me to-morrow, you are not engaged, you'll accept?' At three o'clock we made our appearance in our red uniforms, when Sligo was placed at the left hand of the Queen and I by the Prince Royal .We felt ourselves as much at home as in the dining room at Newbiggin. We had a most excellent dinner of three times four and twenty covers. During dinner the King called out to the Marshal, 'I hope you have claret and champagne for these

Munich

Englishmen; I know them well,' and I can assure you the Marshall took care to offer us enough of it. When we retired to the drawing room the King took us aside and said 'Come I'll show you my wife's apartments, she has some very pretty pictures in them.' Upon which, taking a candle from out of one of the sockets himself, and not permitting any of us to hold it, he carried us through every room, the Queen accompanying him, and pointed out everything which he thought worth our looking at. Many of the Queen's drawings hung on the walls, and a beautiful statue by Canova was in her bedroom. He then said, 'Come and see me to-morrow morning at ten o'clock and I will shew you my own, but mind you come in plain frock coat and boots, otherwise I will not receive you.' Of course we obeyed his summons, and most delighted we were with the beautiful collection of pictures he possesses, and the friendly way in which he told us a vast number of stories connected with them. He then sent for all his little children, the five daughters by his present wife, and shewed them to us with the greatest possible affection, and, upon our taking our leave, he said to us in French, 'I hope you will return to Munich and favour me with two or three days of your company to see the other curiosities which you have not time to look at now.' In fact, he is what in England we call 'a good fellow' and a most excellent country squire, beloved alike by his family and his subjects, and much more fond of horses and of hunting than of performing the duties of a crowned head. As we went out of the room the Prince Royal took me by the hand, gave it a most hearty squeeze and said, 'I only wish that rascal Buonaparte was out of the way, I am sure it would be better both for you and for us,' adding that he hoped we would come to Salzburg where he would be only too happy to welcome us."

Elector Maximilian Joseph, of the house of Wittelsbach, became King of Bavaria after sending his army of 25,000 troops

Munich

in support of the French at the battle of Austerlitz, and bringing Bavaria into the Confederation of the Rhine. 30,000 Bavarian infantry and 2,000 cavalry were contributed to Napoleon's Russian campaign, of whom 68 men survived the retreat from Moscow.

The King abandoned Napoleon shortly before the battle of Leipzig and joined the Sixth Coalition against France.

"So much for Royalty. As for the inhabitants of the town nothing could be kinder than they were. Every house was open to us, and the little societies which we used to meet every evening at Madame Wyfenburgh's, the wife of the Austrian ambassador (who is now in England), were really the most pleasant coteries I ever was at in my life. I can assure you we left Munich with very great regret, but as we have received no letters at all since we left England, we could not possibly stay for longer than ten days. We have only found two packets here, containing your letters Nos. 5 &7; the rest have not yet cast up, but I suppose they will shortly. Here I suppose we shall stay for two or three months, and wait on events which must soon be on the eve of taking place to determine our future course. We are determined to take lodgings, and there is no doubt we shall have an abundance of society, as Count Shakelburg's is the first house in Vienna, where we shall have the entrée and be introduced to the circle.

Amongst the English here is General Airey, a relation of Airey's at Temple Sowerby, but we have not as yet seen him. I will write again by the next courier. I am ashamed of this scrawl, but in fact I have scarcely had a moment to write it, as we have only this instant heard of the opportunity of sending letters. Give my best love to all, and believe me your most affectionate son, William Crackanthorpe.

I am indeed delighted to find you are all well up to the 10th

Munich

December. God bless and preserve you all is my most earnest prayer."

Diary. Munich to Vienna, 9th January, 1814.
"We found a considerable number of persons assembled at the levée of the Prince Royal, to each of whom he said something gracious, and who, their audience finished, retired. Us, however, he desired to stay, saying that he wished to make further acquaintance with the travellers of a nation whom he had always admired and respected alike for her independence and her perseverance. His talk turned chiefly upon the politics of Europe, upon the great changes in the aspect of affairs which the last few months have brought about. Many were his congratulations on the downfall of the power of France, and I must also add, invectives the most bitter against Buonaparte himself. Some of the expressions he used were, I fear, unbecoming a Prince ... No one is better acquainted than Buonaparte with the opinions of each distinguished private individual on the continent, and he is by no means ignorant of the disposition of the Prince Royal towards himself. The Prince told us that he had served during two campaigns under Buonaparte (before Bavaria joined the allied powers), had also spent some time at Paris immediately under the roof of his then chief, and so, he informed us, had had only too many opportunities of making himself acquainted with the real character of the man. He gave many instances of the cruelty and deceit he had witnessed there, confirming the disgust and contempt which he had felt growing in his breast during the two campaigns, Entertaining this opinion (and I have small doubt, expressing it too,) to a man who can never forget or forgive an offence, it is not to be wondered at that Buonaparte should have tried to prevent his succeeding to the Crown. It is

Munich

said that Buonaparte actually wrote to the Emperor of Austria proposing some new arrangement to the exclusion of the Crown Prince, and that this letter was remitted to the King of Bavaria in order to open his eyes as to the conduct of his friend and ally. The line of conduct of the Bavarian kingdom was at once altered, and from this originated that declaration of war which was the beginning of all Buonaparte's late misfortunes. These considerations therefore led us to excuse the extremely strong language of the Crown Prince about a man he had served under as a soldier. The Court at Munich is much inferior in splendour and magnificence to that of Stutgard, where instead of the company being all assembled in one room as here, thirty at least are thrown open each night. But how different are the two Kings! Where the one (the King of Württemberg) forces obedience from his people by terror, the other (the King of Bavaria) draws it from them by mildness, — where the one employs force the other uses love. No man have I ever seen better formed to conciliate the affections of those around him than his Majesty of Bavaria, who unites the dignity of a king with the simplicity of a private individual. Brought up, indeed, as the son of the Duc de Deuxponts, (*Count Palatine of Zweibrücken*) in the service of the French army, and not having been born a king, his manners towards those who are now so much his inferiors are perfect. He seems, as it were, to desire to place everyone upon a level with himself. The Queen, who is sister to the Grand Duke of Baden and to the Empress of Russia, has a sweetness of manner which is extremely fascinating. At first she appears reserved, but after a time this impression fades. To us, as Englishmen, she was most complimentary, speaking for some time on the exertions that England had displayed for the deliverance of Spain, the generous efforts we had made for the independence of Europe, and of our good fortune in having such a general as Lord Wellington …

Munich

Before dinner (the day we dined at the Palace) the King came up to us and said roguishly, in French, 'I beg you will speak English with my wife; she understands it perfectly, but she has not the courage to speak it, and she will be finely confused.' At dinner all was ease and comfort. Each recounted his story, and without the least restraint joined in the general conversation which was going on, or reserved himself for his neighbour, as he liked best.

When taking us around after dinner, the King lamented to us that circumstances should have obliged him to pack up all the pictures in his gallery (a superb collection by the best masters) so that we could not see them. These measures of precaution were, however, absolutely necessary, for, threatened on the one sider by the Austrians (before he had determined to abandon the alliance with France), and afterwards by the French, who, until the battle of Leipzig, had a large 'corps d'observation' posted on his frontier, he had every reason to fear the vengeance of first the one and then the other … The King's private apartments are furnished entirely without pomp or luxury, and are such as might be found in any private house. He had, he told us, appropriated these as being at the top of the castle, and thus enjoying a most extended view, and also, he added, as they were next to those of his children he could have them with him at all times, to amuse him and distract his mind from public affairs. He carried us into his dressing-room in which are the pictures of his first family … Immediately before the King's bed was a bust of Napoleon standing in a most prominent position. He turned to us and said, 'There have I placed the bust of him who has played for the last twenty years *le grand rôle* in Europe. I wish ever to preserve my dread and distrust of him. At the same time,' he added, 'I cannot deny that Buonaparte is a really great man; in any other time or country he would have been out of place. A singular chance has created this man for the very moment suited to his genius, and has further arranged every circumstance to help forward his success' ... The financial state of Bavaria is as bad as it well can be. The taxes amount to above one-third of the income; the value of all produce, land particularly, has much depreciated. The Prime Minister, M. Montgelas, has absolute power, and is more king than the King himself, and I fear he abuses his situation. The army is raised by conscription. The contingent, which, as a member of the Rhine Confederation, it had to furnish, was 30,000 men. At present so great is the enthusiasm for the good cause that no fewer than 70,000 men are ready to take the field. We have had a good opportunity of seeing how quickly men are made into soldiers, and how shortly they are changed from free agents into mere machines. For walking generally towards a great barrack, the court of which was the exercising ground for the new recruits, we used to observe the peasants brought in with all their awkwardness and put into the ranks for the first time, and really in a very few days they are turned out most respectable soldiers."

The Confederation of the Rhine, eventually including every German state except Prussia and Austria, was created by Napoleon in 1806 and the Code Napoléon imposed in 1807. Under it, Bavaria abolished feudal privileges and created judicial equality, but more generally in Germany the Code was considered a failure. The Confederation ceased to exist with the French retreat over the Rhine in November 1813.

"We took our departure with the greatest regret. At the second post village of Stohenlinden we came upon our old friend the Danube, which we had crossed, a mere stream, in the Black Forest, now swelled to a fine navigable river. Along its banks we journeyed, arriving in Vienna on the 9th of January, 1814, very glad to repose ourselves for some time after the perpetual confusion of a three months' journey where all had been so new to us."

By the time they reached Vienna the tensions with Ludolf had led Sligo to suggest that he return. For reasons not specified, "Ludolf is out of favour with all," as Sligo wrote to his mother on 18th January 1814, "and hardly acknowledged by his former acquaintances". He added that he felt sorry for Ludolf but that "it is really unpleasant to have a discounted person with me."

William's Letters. Vienna, January to May 1814.

"Jan. 20th, 1814. Vienna My dear Charlotte, —My mother has, I hope, received the letter which I sent her on the 10th by an English gentleman ... I will now endeavour to give you some idea of how we pass our time here and of the state of society at present in Vienna. We are extremely well lodged in a house overlooking the Danube. We have four excellent apartments, besides rooms for our servants, for which we pay about thirteen guineas a month. The rooms indeed are magnificent and we have every convenience we can desire. By reason of Ludolf's near connexion with the Russian Ambassador we could not, of course, fail to get into the best society of the town. Immediately on our arrival we were asked to an immense dinner party. At present though, in consequence of the war and the enormous expenses entailed by it, there are very few houses open, and little or no gaiety, but a great deal of society on a small scale, which I must confess pleases me much better. The great Austrian families have, it is true, been ever very shy of admitting strangers into their houses, and except to a formal dinner, supper, or ball once a fortnight, you are never admitted within their doors. It is to the Poles therefore that we are indebted for all our hospitality, and great is their kindness I must confess.

I will now give you my diary, which is scarcely or never

Vienna, 1822 by Robert Batty

varied. We breakfast then, all together in the morning, and afterwards each retires to amuse himself as he likes. I, indeed, generally occupy myself till two o'clock with reading and preparing for an Italian master, who comes to me every day, for instead of learning German, which requires so long a time to attain any proficiency, I chose rather a language which is more easy, and also likely to be more useful to me —moreover, the dialect of Vienna is so extremely bad that a Prussian would find as much difficulty in understanding an Austrian as a Cockney the patois of Lancashire. I then amuse myself in looking after the sights till dinner time, which is generally about half-past three in all the houses here. A German dinner, I may inform you, is the very height of sensuality, for it lasts in general at least three hours, one dish following another with the utmost rapidity, till, all being finished, you rise from the table like a crammed turkey, and instead of staying in the drawing room to have some conversation

Vienna

after it, you take your cup of coffee and glass of *liqueur* and immediately retire, so that it appears you come only to eat the dinner and with no other possible object. At six o'clock we get into the carriage, drive round the town and make our calls, which fills up the time till eight o'clock, when you are sure to find a little party assembled together in some house or other for tea. You go without any invitation (provided you have been presented in the house before,) and at ten you all break up, after which I go every night of my life , only having missed once since I came here, to a *petit souper* at the Prince de Ligne's, which lasts till twelve. This is the person some of whose letters Madme. De Stael has published, and the critique of which you may remember in the "Edinburgh Review." He is a man of the most wonderful genius, and has lived in the greatest intimacy with all the leading characters of the last fifty years. You may recollect, perhaps, that he accompanied the Empress Catherine of Russia in her journey to the Crimea, and he has been brought up and lived in all the courts of Europe during his whole life. Nothing, indeed, can be more delightful than is his house, for although extremely poor, he manages to be so hospitable and kind, that independent of the interest you have in his company, you cannot help feeling a great affection for him and a strong regret that circumstances should have been so unfortunate as to deprive him of almost the whole of his property. He has three daughterse, all married, the one as amiable as the other. They come every evening, and, with one or two English, this is the whole party."

Charles Joseph de Ligne, a prince of the Holy Roman Empire, was born in Wallonia in the Austrian Netherlands in 1735. He had a prominent multiple career as soldier, diplomat, letter writer and memorialist, his great reputation resting largely on social fame as the most charming man in Europe. He became an intimate friend of Emperor Joseph II and was made Field

Vienna

Marshal in 1773. During the Napoleonic Wars he lost most of the estate left him by his father, including his home the Château de Beloeil in Wallonia, He lived in Vienna from 1794 and ended his days there, dying in 1814.

"I had forgotten to mention one who is a constant visitor at the Prince de Ligne's, and a very interesting one, the Countess Regivouski. Her mother, the Princess Lubomirski, an attendant upon the late unfortunate Queen of France, underwent the same fate as her mistress, and was guillotined. Her only child was left an orphan, without anyone to take care of her or provide for her existence. The keeper of the prison however, where her mother had been confined, took compassion upon her and brought her up as one of his own children, when by accident one of her relations, who knew that such a child was in existence, happened to be riding past the door where she was attending to some household concerns, either feeding pigs or poultry. He was so struck by her resemblance to her mother that he could not resist making some enquiries about her, and having satisfied himself about her story, had her sent to Poland to her friends and her native country, and thus rescued from the situation in which she was. She now shines as one of the most brilliant characters in Vienna, both as a beauty and a wit. There is also another house which is open in the same way as the de Ligne's, to which *mes compagnons de voyage* go almost as much as I do to the Prince de Ligne's. It is owned by the Duchesse de Sagan, but it does not suit me nearly so well, although in general much more frequented by the English. I am much surprised not to find more of my compatriots assembled here than I have, considering that Austria has been open to us now nearly a year. The only ones whom I think you will know by name are Vernon, a son of the Archbishop of York, Lord Sunderland, and a Mr Trench ... We are kept very much in the background as to what is going in in the political world. All that we know is that the armies are advancing, and that there is no reason why they should not go to Paris. There is, however, but one voice, and that is for peace. Everyone seems tired of the war, and here in Vienna we no longer see the enthusiasm that we found in Prussia and in other parts of Germany. I trust that as my lord Castlereagh has left England it is to procure the blessings of peace, although an idea is afloat that the allies will not treat at all with Buonaparte, but intend to restore the Bourbons to the throne. The south of France is known to be deeply disaffected to him, and the letters which we have seen (coming from the armies) give a most favourable account of the reception of allied forces everywhere there.

I find the climate here much cooler than in England, Ever since we arrived there has been enough snow to put the carriages upon sledges. The gay manner in which the horses are caparisoned and the novel motion of the *traineau* make the exercise quite delightful. Almost every day we take a turn round the Prado, the Hyde Park of Vienna, where all the gay world assemble daily to "see and be seen." As I write, a General O'Reilly has just called upon me. He informs me that it is the undoubted intention of the Emperor of Russia and the King of Prussia to march to Paris, but that the Emperor of Austria will remain in Switzerland. If this is true they seem determined to retaliate upon Buonaparte all the sufferings he has caused to their kingdoms, and, following his example, to dictate peace to him from his own capital. You have no idea how very generally English is spoken in Vienna, so much so that I can sometimes imagine I am in my own country. One family with whom I am very intimate (that of Prince Jablonowsky) really speak it so well that I should never have known them to be foreigners. Upon the whole I can assure you I never felt myself more happy than here, for although, as a nation, they are all envious of us and hate us in

Vienna

their hearts, nevertheless they welcome us so warmly as *individuals* that I should be very ungrateful if I did not feel myself under a great obligation to them for their hospitality."

At some moment since their arrival in Vienna a quarrel broke out between William and Ludolf, who evidently complained of it to Sligo's mother. She in turn wrote to Sligo who answered on 7th February; "As to your remarks relative to the differences between Ludolf and Crackanthorpe there is no use for me to say anything as whatever I might imagine or see you would attribute to my dislike of Ludolf. As to C's being <u>a coarse man</u> I cannot agree with you in that I think him far from it altho' he has not the manner of a petit maître" (*a fop or dandy*) "and in every difference which they had it has been uniformly given against L by all those who have heard the quarrel. All that has now ceased as C has very generously said that nothing should make him quarrel with him as he would thereby spoil the pleasure of the party ...I assure you he takes the Palm among all the Englishmen here. He is sought after in all the finest society in the place ... he intends going thro' Switzerland ..."

On 20th June Sligo reported "Crack has gone to Italy ... we will meet in Naples in October, then to Venice for the carnival"

"I am very sorry to find that the means of communication with England are by no means as easy here as in other parts where we have been, for although we have a *chargé d'affaires* here, yet couriers go so seldom that I fear you may hear neither so constantly nor so regularly from me as I could wish. Be assured, though, that I shall miss no opportunity. Remember me most kindly to all neighbours ... I have kept this letter open till the last moment, but have no fresh news to add. I go this evening to a great ball at Stackelberg's, where I suppose all the world will be assembled. My best love to my mother and Sarah. God bless

Vienna

you all — Your affectionate brother. Wm. Crackanthorpe.

I beg you will tell Sarah that she has put all the buttons upon the necks of my shirts on the wrong side, so that they are extremely inconvenient, and I scold her every time I put them on."

To Sarah

"Vienna, Feb. 16, 1814. My dearest Sarah, My mother's letter and yours of the 12th I received yesterday. You cannot, I assure you, imagine how delightful it is to receive these packets, nor can I describe to you with what anxiety we look forward to the arrival of a courier. Unfortunately, head quarters are, at present, at such an immense distance from this place, that letters make almost the tour of Europe before they come to us. The usual monotony of this town has in some degree been broken in upon, and almost has a spark of enthusiasm been lighted up amongst the Viennois by the announcement of late events. The courier who arrived bearing the dispatches of the victory of Brienne was preceded (according to a very ancient custom, but recently revived) by a troop of forty postilions, all cracking their whips and making the most tremendous noise, after which followed his carriage, and he himself on horseback last of all, the whole going at a foot's pace, and so giving rather the idea of a funeral procession than one announcing joyful tidings. In this triumphal style he made the tour of the whole town, finishing off by depositing his despatches in the *Collège de guerre*. In England we should have published them instantly in an 'Extraordinary' Gazette; here they were not given to the public till the next morning. In the evening we had an illumination, or rather an apology for one, scarcely better than when in London the tradesmen think it right to honour the birthday of any of our Princes of the Blood with a few lamps, in order to secure their custom or to put upon their boards, 'Tallow chandler to his Royal Highness,' etc."

The battle of Brienne was in fact a victory for neither side. 7,000 lives were lost, Blücher was nearly captured and Napoleon briefly surrounded by Cossacks. If it was considered a success in Vienna, the same was true in Paris.

"All sorts of rumours are afloat, immediate peace, the deposition of Buonaparte being the least of them. I cannot myself believe that the spirit of the French is yet so utterly broken that they will allow the allied powers to dictate to them who shall be their sovereign, however much they themselves may wish it.... Throughout the whole Continent one sees nothing but poverty staring one in the face. Every family is lamenting the loss of a child or near relation, or else living in a state of suspense for fear every hour should bring the dreaded intelligence. Yesterday was the birthday of the Emperor, and there was a grand gala at Court, at which almost all the English here made their appearance. Having only a *chargé d'affaires* here, who, according to etiquette, cannot present strangers, we were put under the care of the Grand Chamberlain, who introduced us each separately to the Empress. She has been an extremely pretty woman, but from ill health (and perhaps chagrin) has suffered much in her personal appearance. Her manners, though, are very pleasing, and she said something gracious to each. How different is the Court here to that of London, where, instead of being crammed by thousands into a nasty, dirty, gloomy room in St. James', you pass through a brilliant suite of apartments into the presence chamber, lit with countless wax candles, and magnificent both in its proportions and decorations. About half-past six the Empress entered the room. She was dressed in a most superb gown of Turkish manufacture (red), with a border of sable (a present from the

Charles Joseph, the 7th Prince de Ligne by E.L.

Queen of Sicily), and on her head a tiara of enormous diamonds. Having spoken to the foreign ambassadors the presentation took place, after which she made up her own party, and everyone was free to amuse himself as he liked, either in conversation or play. The great variety of costumes, and the splendour of many of them, made it a most dazzling scene. I especially remarked the Hungarian one. It is hussar, which is the original dress of the country, and the women also wear a national costume too. I fear I shall fail in my description of it! The most striking feature is an apron with an immensely long stomacher composed generally of precious stones. They also wear a long black veil, thrown back from their heads, which is very graceful, the whole quite unique as a Court dress. The display of diamonds exceeded any I had seen at any other Court, for being heirlooms, and handed down from time immemorial, they have gradually accumulated, so that the ladies of the present day may almost cover themselves entirely with them. In England certainly we can boast nothing like them.

I sent Mr. Marriot a long letter, which contained principally an account of a 'chasse' we had at Prince Esterhazy's. Since then nothing remarkable has occurred. The same routine of houses visited every evening. I am at length become (if I dare praise myself) so great a favourite of the de Ligne family that I never miss going there any one night. I cannot give you an adequate description of their excellent qualities or of their kindness to me. I find the very best society there, so that as a school both for manners and French it cannot be excelled."

The Prince de Ligne and his daughters perhaps appreciated in William a candour without guile, a keen sensibility to impressions, and interests somewhat less worldly than those, for example, that came more naturally to Sligo.

"The weather is bitterly cold and very changeable. At

Vienna

present we are waiting for a little frost in order that we may make a little tour in Hungary, a country but little known to the English. We shall go along the banks of the Danube to Buda , and return by Kemnetz, a tour which can easily be accomplished in a week or ten days. What we shall do in the spring is wholly uncertain, and will in great measure depend on public events. The most interesting part of Europe is now however open to us. Affairs in Italy seem all satisfactorily arranged, and I believe at this moment there would be no difficulty in going direct to Naples. The Tyrol and Switzerland, however, just now fill our minds …

I regret extremely I cannot send you this time a more interesting letter, but as for political news you know everything so much sooner in England than we do that I never think of it … We have had a new arrival in Lord Dumfries from St. Petersburg, who we find a great acquisition. And now goodbye. With my best love to my mother and Charlotte, — Your affectionate brother, Wm. Crackanthorpe."

Letter to his mother

"Vienna, March 1st, 1814. My dear Mother —It is a long time since we had letters from England, owing, I suppose, to the long round they have to take by Châtillon, before they are forwarded to us. I trust some are coming immediately, as I knows no happiness so great as that of getting letters from Newbiggin.

Of public events I can tell you but little. I believe no people in the world are kept in the dark so much as the good inhabitants of Vienna. The Press indeed, the continent over, is entirely subject to a Government censor, who never allows anything to appear in a public print but what suits the allies, so that save by a whisper sometimes, we never hear of a loss or misfortune that may have befallen them. It would seem, though, as if something serious

Vienna

had happened, otherwise Headquarters would never have retired and all the detachments have been called in. We know nothing, either, as to how the negotiations are going forward. There are many rumours, but they are circulated for commercial purposes. There is only one wish here and that is for peace, and indeed for my part I know not what they are now fighting for, if it is true that Buonaparte has accepted their terms. As for driving him from the throne of France in order to re-establish the Bourbons, that will never succeed in the long run. It is true that in some parts of the country the French are extremely discontented with the existing Government, but such have been the excesses committed by the invading armies (he inevitable consequences of war) that, we hear from Châtillon, the spirit of the people is considerably changed, and it is impossible to say what form it may take. Since every nation desires peace, I cannot conceive why it is not made.

Sligo, I am sorry to say, is become sadly *ennuyé* of his stay here, and talks of setting out this month upon an expedition in which I do not care to join him. He wishes to endeavour again to make his way to Headquarters in France. Now I really can conceive nothing more foolish, but having taken the idea into his head, there is no possibility of persuading him to abandon it. For myself, I must confess, I have seen enough of the horrors and miseries of war, and desire to see no more. Pestilence and famine are, we hear, raging in the neighbourhood of the troops in the most dreadful way, and although by taking precaution one may escape oneself, I cannot understand the pleasure in seeing a whole population scourged and laid low by them. Sligo and Ludolf, then, may set out that way and traverse a country (which they have seen as far as Schaffhausen) in this delightful season when the thermometer is 12 degrees below freezing point. I shall stay quietly here till the spring, and give them the meeting again somewhere in the north of Italy. I shall not be alone, for Lord

Vienna

Dumfries and Mr. Baillie, both of whom I knew at Cambridge, are going the same route, and we shall journey together when the time comes. In my opinion it is little less than madness to think of undertaking a journey of pleasure in such a season. Moreover, nothing can be more agreeable than this town, and I see not the wisdom of exchanging a certain pleasure for an undoubted misery. I shall remain for a month or five weeks longer, till the leaves make their appearance on the trees."

This account does not quite correspond with the twofold explanation given by Sligo to his mother of the difference that arose between him and William. Writing on the 26th of February he reported that Crackanthorpe had refused to go with him to Paris as his "Brougham-ish politics have now got to such a height that he says he could not bear to see the finest nation in the world invaded by a parcel of Scythians."

Further on Sligo added, in the same frank manner with his mother that he used in writing of his own affairs, that "Crackanthorpe is desperately in love and will remain in Vienna."

William continued —

"I have been offered a house by the Prince de Ligne if I choose to occupy it. It is part of an old convent, and most delightfully situated upon a hill overlooking the whole country. Here he and his family retire during the summer months, each occupying a *maisonette,* of which there are about twenty, containing three small rooms, two for yourself and one for your servant, all fitted up most nicely. One of them, somewhat larger, is made into a dining room, where you are all expected to meet at the dinner hour, whilst the rest of the day is entirely at your own disposal. Some twenty or thirty people so assemble, forming the most delightful society, all guests of the Prince de Ligne.

Nothing of interest has happened since I last wrote, except

Vienna

that we have been very much lately at Prince Starhemberg's, who was formerly Austrian ambassador at St. James's. His house is quite after the English style, for having lived 19 years in England it is not to be wondered at that he should desire to adopt its comfortable customs. His financial affairs are, unfortunately, in a very bad way. This is the case, though, with half of the great Austrian families. The establishment of Prince Esterhazy was reduced the other day (he has perhaps the most extensive possessions of any private individual in Europe), 829 servants of different descriptions were turned off. This will give you an idea of the extravagant style of living of this Hungarian Prince. The Liechtenstein family too, which comes next in point of wealth, is also very embarrassed. Vienna now depends almost entirely upon strangers for its gaiety.

When Sligo goes I must draw the drafts in my own name. Will you have the goodness to tell Messrs. Martin and Stone to answer them; the money to be paid to my account and not to Sligo's, as, by mistake, it has hitherto been? The weather is intolerably cold, and it is impossible to walk with any pleasure. I have the satisfaction, however, of thinking you are little better off in England, for I see the snow has been so thick that communication between the capital and the counties has been stopped. Some of your letters are still missing. In your last, however, you told me you are all well, and that is the most important point for me to know. My best love to my sisters. God preserve you all. — Your affectionate son, Wm.Crackanthorpe."

Letter to Charlotte.

"Vienna, March 5th, 1814.
… Sligo sets out tomorrow, which I think extremely rash . There is, however, no dissuading him, and … I must leave him to make the best of it. I shall meet him somewhere in Lombardy, possibly

Vienna

at Verona. This sad news of Blücher's defeat has lowered our spirits greatly. Headquarters, it would seem, are undoubtedly retired to Langres."

During the so called Six Days Campaign from 19th to 14th February Napoleon, by rapid tactical brilliance and with a small force largely of young conscripts, inflicted four defeats on Blücher's allied army threatening Paris, and forced him to suspend his advance.

"We must keep our courage, and hope for the best. All accounts from France give a most miserable account of that wretched country — exhausted alike in provisions and in men. The effort which Buonaparte has made is indeed marvellous. Your letter (No. 13) reached me yesterday. You ask me my plans. I intend to go down to Rome, and perhaps to Naples. I trust, however, long before I reach those places to have met with Sligo. I only lament that he will not enter Italy by the best road for a traveller ..."

Letter to Sarah.

"Vienna, March 10th, 1814.
... Since Sligo set out I have been alone, Ludolf having migrated to the house of some friends here. I have moved to a smaller lodging, and am as comfortable as possible. The kindness and friendship I meet with is quite inconceivable. Of the goodness of the Viennois to all Englishmen I have had a most convincing proof. Poor Percival, a son of Lord Arden's, has been ill here for some time, and he has been taken care of by a family, with whom I am intimate, as if he had been one of their own sons. Every day they have been to see him, and they have supplied him from their own kitchen with everything which could tempt his appetite. (At present, poor fellow, I am happy to say, he is better.) We (Lord Dumfries and I) propose to set out on our route to Italy on the 1st

Vienna

of May, going by Styria, Croatia, and Istria. Vienna we have pretty well seen now. Schönbrunn, the palace of the Emperor, where he spends part of the summer, is an immense pile of building, in the very worst taste possible, surrounded by Dutch gardens, kept in the worst order, and most neglected. We, however, had a most amusing party there the other day, taking our dinners with us and eating them in one of the greenhouses.

I fear one of my letters to you must have got lost, as the gentleman to whom it was confided has been robbed on the road of everything he possessed, as also of the despatches given him by Mr. Lambe, our chargé d'affaires here. I hear from Sligo, who passed through Munich the other day, that the King received him in just the same hospitable manner at dinner, and gave him his portrait on Sligo's taking his leave. I have just seen a compatriot who has come from Headquarters at Troyes. He gives a wretched account of the misery prevailing there — no provisions to be obtained and the country exhausted. From what he tells me I am thankful I am not with Sligo, as I am sure it is a scheme which will be as disagreeable as it is foolish. He tells me that an universal apathy prevails; that the terror they have of the Cossacks is beyond all imagination; and that the Bourbons are completely forgotten. I do not pretend to understand the game the allies are playing, and if it be true that the opportunity for making peace is now gone by, I only fear we shall have a second Spain, and that in fact it will become a war of extermination. The prayer for peace is here universal. We have had an addition to our society in the arrival of Lord Gower, just arrived from Berlin. He brings us report of the probability of a marriage between the Duke of Cumberland and a Princess de Solms, who is quite as bad as he in every respect, so there is a pretty prospect of happiness and morality between them!

We are now in the midst of Lent, *jours de pénitence*. All

Vienna

dancing is forbidden, and in its stead *Comédies de Salon* are substituted. A little French play is given every week at some house or other, and certainly the acting of them is perfection. Send letters still to Grafton Street, for as Sligo will be at Headquarters, he will forward them to me as soon as they reach him. It is now long since I had any news, but so uncertain are the communications with Vienna that this must not be wondered at. Do not, therefore, be uneasy if you do not hear regularly. No opportunity shall escape me of writing …"

Letter to his mother.

"Vienna, April 7th, 1814.
… It is an age since I had letters from you, and could I not attribute it to the circumstance of my letters having gone with Sligo's to headquarters, I should have been extremely unhappy.

The position of affairs begins to create very unpleasant sensations, and the spirits of the people are now very different to what they were a month ago. You hear now no vaunting of a triumphal entry into Paris; instead there is considerable apprehension about the safety of the allied armies. Buonaparte's military talents have, I fear, shewn themselves too great for the slow and tardy movements of the Germans. The effect, indeed, which these ill-tidings have produced on the paper circulation of the country is lamentable, the proportion being raised from 2 to 1 to nearly 3 and a half to 1 in the course of a few days, i.e. where we formerly got 14 florins for £1 sterling, we now get 23 and 24; so that all those unfortunate people who are Government servants, or have their rents paid in paper, lose more than one-third of their income. Every article of consumption is, of course, raised in proportion as the exchange falls. I wonder how people in England would like this! It is quite possible, too, that the paper money will actually become of no value whatever, and the consequence of this, if it occurs, I do not know. The distresses which the war has caused are without example. In the province of Styria alone there are at present 300 estates under sequestration by the Government, in consequence of their owners being unable to pay the taxes. I saw yesterday a letter from a lady at Grätz in which she says, 'I have paid 36 per cent upon my income, besides all the contributions which have been levied on my estate, they having taken away all the corn and hay which it produced for the army. I am now under the necessity of selling my carriage horses, not because I want the money, but because I have no means of nourishing them, nor can I obtain any around. I had nothing left but two little ponies which my son and I used to ride, and these were put into requisition the other day to drag cannon into Italy.' France is suffering most horribly. She has surely been most amply repaid for the horrors she has inflicted on other nations. However, this does not appear to be her own idea or policy, or the recent negotiation at Châtillon would not have failed. Most assuredly Buonaparte will not make peace now till either the allies are the other side of the Rhine or he himself is laid low.

This is the *Semaine Sainte.* It is observed in the most strict and scrupulous manner; every house is shut, except to particular friends. I can assure you the rigid manner in which many have fasted during Lent begins to shew itself in their countenances. Only one meal a day is permitted, and it is generally *maigre,* without either breakfast or supper, so that the other day when I was out with a lady she actually fell down from weakness, unable to support herself from having fasted so long.

We, Lord Dumfries and I, start on the 2nd of May. We shall begin by Hungary, and then turn down to Fiume and Trieste, when we shall immediately make for Rome. Lord Gower and Mr. Vernon set out to-morrow upon nearly the same expedition, and all the English will be leaving Vienna very shortly. I am filled

Vienna

with regret at leaving Vienna. Most of my friends, too, I can hardly hope to see again, but most especially do I regret leaving the old Prince de Ligne, who has been my best friend here, and who is really the life and soul of the place ...

I just now hear that the allies have entered Paris. *If this be true,* the end of the war cannot be far distant. I am very sorry to see the account of the death of poor Colonel Carleton in the unfortunate attack on Bergen op Zoom. Have the goodness to say everything that is kind for me to the Askham family upon the melancholy event ...

What has become of Sligo since he entered France I know not, for I have had no letters from him for three weeks. I trust he has not been made prisoner, as has happened to another man I know making the same expedition. Still send your letters to Grafton Street, as they will be forwarded by Lord Aberdeen, who will send them after me to the first place I can rely upon staying any time after I leave Vienna (which I do not look forward to with any great satisfaction). *Mais ce n'est que le premier pas qui coûte.* Young Graham, of Netherby, is just arrived here from Naples."

On 31st March French forces surrendered in Paris. On April 6th Napoleon signed an unconditional abdication. On the 28th he sailed for Elba, and on the 30th the Treaty of Paris ended the War of the Sixth Coalition..

"Vienna, April 24th, 1814.

My dear Mother, — What a strange revolution has taken place in the order of things since I last wrote to you! Thank God affairs have taken the turn they have, the scourge by which Europe has so long been chastened no longer exists, and she may look for the blessings of a long and happy peace. I would indeed almost that I was in France at this moment, but at the same time

Vienna

I cannot bring myself to go amongst a people whom I at present so much despise ... There will be now such an inundation of English at Paris that Dumfries and I are determined to go to see Italy first, so on May 2nd we start by Hungary, going down by Fiume and Grätz. Venice will be open, as also all the tows in Lombardy, and the Pope has returned to Rome.

Sligo was a little premature in his departure from Vienna! I had a letter the other day from him giving me an account of his misfortunes, for which I do not in the least compassionate him. Having procured passports to Headquarters he was on the road to Chaumont when he was informed that all the corps diplomatique were to arrive there shortly. Too happy of course to meet his compatriots he awaited their arrival, but no sooner had they eaten their dinner together than an alarm came that the French were advancing on the town. This put them all to flight. Sligo had no horses and was unable to get any, and was thus compelled to abandon his carriage with all his property. He could only save his portfolio. If Lord Aberdeen had not been so kind as to give him a seat in his carriage he would probably have had the pleasure of seeing the inside of a French prison (not the most agreeable spot in the world). I congratulate myself that I was not with him. I should have lost everything. Sligo could not save even a single clean shirt. Vienna is emptying fast. Its inhabitants are wiser than Londoners, for they all begin to pack up for the country directly the fine weather comes ... I have just come from the Cathedral, where a *Te Deum* has been sung. The Empress and all the Court were present. The cortege on such an occasion is most splendid. The Hungarian Guard, which surrounded the Empress, is composed of young noblemen clad in the most superb uniforms, and mounted on white Arabian horses. After I leave this place I shall not expect any more letters from you till I reach Rome. We are well fortified with letters of introduction

Vienna

for almost all the great towns in Italy. At Rome we shall be most particularly recommended to a Prince Poniatowski, whose house is the best in the town for strangers, as also to a Princess Czartoryska, whose daughter is married and living here. We are here just one month forward in vegetation than you in England. The oaks are pretty much in the same state as about 29th of May with you. Give my best love to Charlotte and Sarah, and believe me your most affectionate son, Wm. Crackanthorpe."

To Sarah. 27th April, 1814.
"The return of the Emperor is eagerly looked for. Report says that it is his intention to pay you a visit in England, along with the Emperor of Russia, to assist at the marriage of the young Princess. But I do not believe it; it may suit Alexander of Russia very well, but by no means the cold and phlegmatic temper of the Austrian Emperor. Nor do I think he can be in spirits for such an undertaking. The unfortunate and miserable lot of his daughter has made too deep an impression upon him to allow him to enjoy *fêtes* of any kind. Her lot is indeed pitiable, sacrificed in the first instance by her father in order that he might preserve his empire, and now torn away from her husband (whom it is said she really loved) in order to obtain an establishment for her son. But what a glorious game Schwarzenberg played, and worthy indeed is he of the honours awaiting him. I heard yesterday a charming trait of his disinterestedness. After the entry into Paris the Emperor of Russia came to him and said, 'What is there I can do for you to reward you? Ask what you will and I will grant it.' Upon which the Prince replied, 'Replace, then, General Wittgenstein in the favour he deserves, he is a brave man and merits your Majesty's protection.' (Wittgenstein had been disgraced by reason of a little caprice of the Emperor's.) Thereupon he was made a field

Vienna

marshal. After the battle of Leipzig, Schwarzenberg shewed the same generosity ...

On our way to Buda we shall stay a few days with Count Esterhazy, and I will endeavour to send you some little description of our visit there ...

Vienna, May 4th, 1814.

... I was delighted to receive a great packet of your letters from Sligo, which contained the one you wrote to me on the 28th of March. I find by it that the KirkbyThore Common is enclosed, and that great exertions must have been made to have done it so quickly. I trust my farm at Hale is exempt from the tithe, if not (if I recollect rightly) my estate will not be liable to any of the expenses attending the enclosure. The Act was so carelessly drawn up that the same words by which there was a possibility of excluding my farm from participating in the full benefit of the Act would also save it from all expenses. Be so good, therefore, as to speak with Mr. Graves on the subject, and as I am sure you will show more judgement in disposing of the new land than I should, I beg you will use your own discretion, for which I give you full powers ... The Archduchess (the wife of Buonaparte) is expected here in a few days. She will occupy the palace of Schönbrunn, a mile from Vienna, where all the Court moves shortly to give her the meeting. What a miserable lot is hers ... Vienna is nearly empty. The English colony have dispersed, and most of the Viennese ladies have gone to Paris to meet their husbands, who are now enjoying a little rest after this dreadful war. This letter will go as usual to Sligo. I know well it contains nothing interesting, except the assurance that I was never better in my life, and I would not lose the opportunity of telling you that. I am glad to see Charlotte writes you are as blooming as

Pressburg

ever. May you ever continue so, and with best love to my sisters, your affectionate son, Wm. Crackanthorpe.

Diary. Vienna to Venice. May to July.

"Having lost my first *compagnon de voyage,* Sligo, I thought myself extremely happy in meeting with Lord Dumfries, whose route and ideas corresponded so nearly with my own. We agreed to begin by a little tour in Hungary, and on the 14th May left Vienna, and directed our route towards Pressburg. My sorrow (at leaving Vienna) was increased by the idea of the more than probability that I should never again see many of those whom I had loved the most, and both for Dumfries and myself this idea was sufficient, for some days, to damp the pleasure of travelling for us … In consequence of the tardy obstinacy of our postilions we were eight hours on the road between Vienna and Pressburg. We used every kind of threat and entreaty, but to no purpose, so at last we came to the determination to pay them only the bare sum commanded by the post *ordonnance,* and this gratification of the passion of revenge was the only particle of pleasure we had on the journey!

At Pressburg we stayed a day and a night. In the Castle are at present some French prisoners, part of the late garrison of Dresden. With many of these men we entered into conversation. We asked them various questions about the events which had happened in France about which they seemed quite ignorant, except that they understood that 'Louis Bourbon', as they called him, had been placed on the throne, and that Napoleon was no longer Emperor. With one voice they all said that he (Napoleon) was the greatest captain and warrior of his age, and that had it not been for his misfortunes in Russia he would have been utterly invincible.

The day which we passed at Pressburg happened to be

Pressburg

Sunday, and a *fête* in celebration of the liberation of the Pope was fixed for it. The whole town was abroad and universal gaiety prevailed. I was most amused by a corps of young cadets — children actually of 8 to 14 years old —the sons of soldiers of the regiment, who, all dressed *à l'Hongroise,* with all the regular military equipments, went through the manoeuvres with absolute precision. The plan is adopted throughout the whole of the Hungarian army, certain funds being set aside by each regiment for the education of the children, who are thus trained from their very infancy to the use of arms. In the evening we attended the *fête*. The amusements were all extremely innocent; dancing, music, skittles, and roundabouts, all conducted with the greatest harmony. Drunkenness is never seen at these village festivals; good humour and decency reign, so that to see the recreation of these people who labour so hard during the rest of the week is delightful.

The next day, when we were about to set off, we called for the bill, but were so astonished by its enormity that we thought it absolutely necessary to endeavour to bring the landlord to reason. In this attempt, however, we utterly failed, and the imposition being too gross to be supported, we resolved to make an application to the burgomaster. We thereupon went to him and found him an extremely well informed, honest, and polite man, speaking five languages (English amongst them). He readily listened to our complaint, and afforded us a just redress, for, calling up our landlord, he gave him a most wholesome lecture upon the infamy of his conduct. And, having reduced the amount of the bill considerably, he thanked us for having given him an opportunity of showing us he did his duty ...

On leaving Pressburg we passed through Nitra, a considerable town of about 6,000 inhabitants, most of whom appeared to be Jews. An air of poverty met us on all sides. Many of the houses were in ruins; the people in rags and dirt and filthiness everywhere. It is the seat of an episcopal see. The Bishop's palace is in the interior of the fortress, which is guarded by his own troops, kept at his own expense, and clothed according to his own taste. He exercises the full rights of a sovereign, and the peasants are entirely committed to his mercy. We were shown the prison in which these poor creatures are confined, as also the instruments of punishment which are used upon them. All this part of the kingdom of Hungary is peopled by Slavons or Slovacks, as they are called, the descendants of the ancient Sarmatii. In their religious opinions they are pretty nearly equally divided, one half being Catholic and the other half Lutheran. The numbers of the Lutherans has in some degree diminished, for, notwithstanding the unlimited toleration which the law enforces, things are made as difficult for them as possible in every way.

    The greater proportion of the nobles are Catholics, so that the Lutheran clergy are entirely dependent on their flock, who are all far from rich. The Government gives them nothing. It must, nevertheless, be remarked that their schools are much better kept up and the people have more information generally than can be found amongst the Catholic population … The houses of the Slovacks are universally built of clay and whitewashed. Their appearance is almost that of savages; both sexes having their heads greased with lard, and their uncombed locks hanging about their dark complexioned faces. The men's costume consists of blue pantaloons with top boots, a short chemise of coarse linen reaches the waist which is encircled by a large leathern girdle; a vest made of sheepskin with all the wool upon it, and an immense mantle of white cloth is thrown over their shoulders. The costume is completed by an enormous broad-brimmed hat. The women are very similarly attired. They have a white petticoat with a bright coloured body, and in winter a sheepskin like the men. If unmarried, they wear their hair hanging down in a long plaited cue; if married, it is turned up (a never failing mark of distinction this). They, too, universally wear top boots ... The whole of this country has been famous for its mines of gold, silver, and lead. Some of the mines near Kremnitz date from the time when it was a Roman province. At present they are very poor, the output of the metal hardly covering the cost of getting it. There are, however, about 4,800 miners employed, who receive about 8 florins a fortnight in wages. This amounts to about 12s. of our money, and out of it they are obliged to find the powder they use for blasting, as also all their tools. All Jews are forbidden to inhabit this district so that no traffic or chicanery by the workmen can be carried on ... The works are, indeed, enormous, the whole of the mountain on which the town is built being undermined, so that one may travel for miles underground in a labyrinth; some of the miners, in fact, are an hour and a half in arriving at their place of work. We had some difficulty in making ourselves understood, as none of us spoke German fluently, and our only means of communicating with the inspectors who accompanied us was in Latin, which they spoke with the same fluency as their own native tongue. All affairs are conducted in Latin. I was glad that, though I could not reply, never having been accustomed to speak Latin, I could understand them (though somewhat ashamed of my ignorance!)

Neusohl, an episcopal town through which we passed, is remarkable only for its extreme dirtiness. In the centre of the Grande Place is piled the accumulated filth of years, no means being ever used to clean it. And here we were unexpectedly detained a whole week in consequence of Dumfries having a sudden attack of fever, which prevented our going forward. Shut

Neusohl

up in a miserable vaulted chamber, the walls of which had not been whitewashed for the last century, containing for all furniture, one table, a few old chairs, and two little straw beds, our situation was not a very enviable one. Our servants, too, made themselves understood with the greatest difficulty, few of the people speaking German, and everything being on the poorest scale. Had it not been for the hospitality and kindness of the Baron de Riva, I do not know what we should have done. He was so good as both to open his house to us and to offer whatever we needed for Dumfries's illness.

During our stay we saw one of the curious Catholic festivals, namely, a pilgrimage to a shrine dedicated to the Virgin, in a most retired part of the mountains. We saw thousands of peasants, collected in bands according to the district whence they came, each preceded by crucifix and chanting a hymn to a most simple and impressive air. The men were bareheaded, and all, of both sexes, were without shoes and stockings. They carried provisions for some days on their backs. At every image and crucifix they met with by the road side they dropped *en masse* upon their knees, no matter how dirty it might be, whilst repeating a certain number of Pater Nosters. Under one of our windows happened to be placed one of these images, so we witnessed this remarkable sight close at hand.

Upon leaving Neusohl we had the same trouble with our host as at Pressburg. He desired to charge us the enormous sum of 250 florins for the miserable fare and lodgings we had in his house during the time we had been so unluckily detained. We felt we could not put up with such an imposition, and I therefore made an application to my friend, the Baron, who, with his usual kindness, arranged the matter for us. He reduced the bill to 88 florins, which he said was even thus too much. Throughout the whole of Hungary we found the same disposition to cheat strangers amongst the innkeepers and postmasters. They are a set of creatures, who, calling themselves *nobiles Hungarici*, live upon the little pension the place affords. This being barely sufficient to support them they resort to all the tricks they can invent to gain a few extra florins. They enjoy many of the privileges of the great magnates. They have the same power over the peasants (whom they oppress grievously), and they are much too fine gentlemen to do what is actually their duty ... and as there is no remedy, the traveller is often obliged to wait hours, and even days, till it suits their pleasure to furnish him with post horses."

Letter to Sarah.

"Neusohl, May 26, 1814. My dear Sarah, — Dumfries is now nearly quite recovered, and I trust we shall set out tomorrow. I have found Hungary even more interesting than I had imagined. It is peopled by two different races, the Slavons or Slovacks, as they are called, and the Germans. The Slavons being extremely prolific will in time drive out the Germans. Their language is nearly the same as Russian. Luckily for us Dumfries has with him one of the poor French prisoners whom he picked up in Moscow. This man acts as a kind of interpreter, as he has picked up a little of the language. The peasants throughout the whole of Hungary are a very fine race. But they are kept in the most miserable state of subjection by the nobles. They are only looked upon as brutes, and although they are not actually bought and sold with the land, as in Russia, they are in a most degraded condition. Unable to possess a single acre of land, they have to submit with patience to the caprice and tyranny of the landowners. All rents are paid in kind or in service, and so great is the power of the 'lord' that he can confine them in his castle and inflict corporal punishment

Neusohl

Graz, 1842, by Kolb

on them without judge or jury.

When at Pressburg we called on the Princess de Rohan, whom we had known at Vienna. She is the widow of the unfortunate Duc d'Enghien, who was so barbarously assassinated by Buonaparte. The marriage was never publicly acknowledged, as she was not of royal blood. If her husband had lived, most probably she would have shared his honours and been received as his wife. She is a most interesting and charming woman, and merits a better lot.

The country around is most lovely, and it frequently recalls to me the scenery around our northern lakes. The manners of the people are still simple, and hospitality prevails throughout, which is delightful. We never stop at a post-house without an offer of milk and bread being made to us. The famous wine of Tokay is made here, and if the roads had been a little better, and had Dumfries been strong enough, I think we should have paid those noted vineyards a visit. My very best love to my mother and Charlotte. — Ever your most affectionate brother, Wm. Crackanthorpe."

Letter to Charlotte.

"Gratz, June 18th, 1814. My dear Charlotte — We are arrived here safe and sound. Dumfries has quite lost the ague which plagued him so in Hungary. We stayed a night on our way here at Chacwar, another château of Esterhazy's. He forwarded us on by his horses to Pepa, a distance of 80 English miles. During the whole of those 80 miles we passed only through this one man's estates, which produce what in England would be £100,000 a year. Here we entered the great road and then proceeded on to Furstenfeld, a little town on the frontier, where we took our leave of Hungary, never, I fancy, to see it more. Our route has been well chosen, for we have seen all that is most beautiful and most interesting in the country. I must say that the impression which Hungary has left upon my mind is not the most favourable, and I shall not desire to pay it a second visit.

We have found here a compatriot in the Comtesse de Purgstall, whose son has a magnificent estate close by. She is a sister, I believe, of the present Lord Cranstoun, and much resembles Mrs. Brougham, as she speaks with the same broad Scotch accent, and she has all that sweetness of manner for which the latter is remarkable."

Mrs. Elena Brougham was the mother of Henry Brougham the great Whig reformer and Lord Chancellor from 1830 to 1834. She was a niece of the historian William Robertson, Principal of

Fiume

the University of Edinburgh.

"We have passed two days entirely in her house, which she has made as agreeable as possible by inviting all those people to meet us whom she thought we would like. She also lent us her carriage to visit the château which the ci-devant King of Westphalia is going to occupy. Some of his equipages were already arrived, and we were amused at seeing the crown and initials still retained on them. He assumes the title of Comte de Hartz, and has a suite of 60 persons, a pretty strong proof that he has taken pretty good care to provide well for himself.

The Emperor was to make his entrée into Vienna today. Great preparations have been made and the illuminations alone were to cost about £130,000 of our current money. The little King of Rome has, I hear, won the hearts of all the ladies at Vienna; never was seen so charming a boy and all are in love with him. Amongst the anecdotes told of him is what he said to the Prince de Ligne, who had been, in full uniform, to pay his court to the Archduchess. The little fellow remarked on his Field Marshal's uniform, and immediately asked 'Whether it was one of those Marshals who had deserted his dear papa.' I must now close this short letter, for the post only leaves here twice a week."

Letter to his mother,

Fiume, June 26th, 1814.
"Whilst I am waiting for a fair wind to embark I must bring down my journal from the time I left Gratz. We passed through Lower Styria. A most lovely and rich country, into Croatia, which is inhabited by a race of men who, from their neighbourhood to the Turks, are ever engaged in petty warfare. They are a race of men who think of nothing but plunder and pillage. Consequently all

Fiume

agriculture is neglected; the women do all the labour of the fields, whilst the men pass their time either in complete idleness, herding a few cattle, or else in predatory raids into Bosnia. The same scenes take place as formerly upon our borders between the English and the Scotch. The high roads are now become quite unsafe for travellers in consequence of the numbers of these fellows but lately returned from the wars, and also from the bad police administration. We, however, have luckily escaped. I trust the Government will adopt the same strong measures as the French, who in one county alone shot two hundred of them in six months ... The road from Carlstadt to Fiume, a distance of 90 miles is really one of the wonders of the world. Passing over a chain of mountains, 2632 feet above the sea level at its highest point, it is so beautifully engineered that the ascent or descent in any one place is hardly perceptible. It cost upwards of five millions, and it is a speculation of a company of private individuals. The forests which it traverses are enormous, and the only profit derived from them are the acorns, on which the pigs are fed, and the skins of the wolves which infest them, as there are no means of selling the wood.

Here, as elsewhere, the taxes levied are enormous, in some cases amounting to half the income, and examples are not wanting where the *whole* has been taken by the Government. All the world here speaks Italian, and you can have no idea how sincerely I congratulate myself that I have no more to do with the sleepy Germans. Here everyone is civil and attentive, not perhaps less rascals than the others, but all their knavery is managed with so much adroitness that when one discovers it one cannot help laughing at their ingenuity ... The peasantry are the finest race I ever saw, the women particularly beautiful, and all dressed (the coiffure of each different) with so much neatness and taste that the contrast with their German sisters is quite

Map of Italy, 1815, by A Findlay, published by Thomas Kelly

delightful. The skies are the deepest blue, fruit of all kinds abound, in fine, all the luxuries of life — that of cleanliness excepted — are to be had at very moderate cost. I cannot yet like their cookery. Butter has totally disappeared, and everything is dressed in oil.

The same want of money prevails at Trieste. There reigns throughout the country such an air of poverty that one might really have thought one was in the Highlands of Scotland rather than in a country abounding in the luxuries of life. Wine and oil they have in profusion, but all commerce was put an end to under the French system, and vineyards and olives alike are totally neglected.

I am sorry to see by the newspapers that the unpleasant affair between the Prince and Princess of Wales is again renewed. I was in hopes after the last inquiry it might have rested quiet. I am sure if the Prince knew his own interests he would have let it remain so. You can have no idea how bitterly everyone here expresses himself against the Prince, and how much he lowers himself by such conduct in the eyes of the whole world. I dare not indeed repeat to you all I hear upon the subject."

The Prince of Wales was actively seeking information about his wife's adulteries on her travels, with a view to persuading Ministers – as he later did – to bring a process of divorce in Parliament. This was defeated in the House of Lords by Henry Brougham in one of his most brilliant forensic performances.

"The day after tomorrow we go hence to Venice, where I trust we shall arrive in three days. We shall stay some time to see all its curiosities. Of society I believe there is not much.

Venice

The Doge's Palace and Grand Canal, Venice, from Prout's 'Continental Tourist'

Letter to Charlotte.

"Venice, July 7th, 1814.
My dear Charlotte, — Such is the variety of sights, of works of art, and of curiosity which now begin to crowd in upon us, that I find it impossible to keep a regular journal, or indeed to give you any adequate description of this wonderful city of Venice. All other cities indeed more or less resemble each other, but this rising out of the waves and having canals for its streets offers a magical spectacle. To those who knew it under its ancient government it is scarcely to be recognised, for it presents at this moment a sad picture of fallen greatness. Still it is perhaps more rich in works of art than any other city in the world (Paris excepted), and how long it would take to see them all as they should be seen I cannot say. Let me endeavour to tell you of a

Venice

few of those things that struck me the most. Upon my entrance to the Place de St. Marc, where all travellers make their début, I was quite struck dumb with astonishment. Each side of the vast square is surrounded by the Palace of the Doge and the Church of St. Mark filling one end, the whole enclosed by an arcade, which is the promenade of the town. The church is magnificently built in the Greek style, and over the central door are the four bronze horses which the Venetians stole from Constantinople.

The ancient Palace of the Doge is now converted into government offices, Buonaparte having chosen to make himself a new residence out of the houses of the *Procurators* and the famous *Salle des nobles*. All the pictures which formerly adorned this last have been transferred to Paris. The immense number of marble palaces, residences of private individuals, gives one the best idea of the wealth of this town. Their interiors are even more rich than their exteriors, being all fitted up with the richest brocade and silks, their ceilings painted by Raphael or some other of the first masters. In seeing them one imagines that their possessors must have all the wealth of Golconda to have applied to. But, unfortunately, this is not the case; the owners of these beautiful palaces often know not where to seek a dinner, and such is their distress that should they have the misfortune to break a window it must so remain, as they cannot afford to repair it. Most of the palaces are abandoned, twenty-two, indeed, have been actually razed to the ground, and many are sinking into a state of ruin … The gondolas are all covered with black, according to an ancient decree of the Republic, to prevent the immense luxury which the citizens went to in fitting them up. The gondoliers are a magnificent race of men; very adroit in the management of their boats. Frequently they sing you whole stanzas of Tasso whilst rowing. Their numbers are sadly diminished. The gondoliers of private individuals used formerly to amount to above three thousand, now they are not above 250.

Many of the Venetian nobles are actually reduced to ask alms in the streets, and at every moment some woman, covered with a black veil (to prevent her being known), presents herself for your charity. The Arsenal is very fine. I do not mean to compare it to Portsmouth, but it is well worth a visit. Unfortunately, though, the Bucentaur, the most beautiful and rich vessel ever built, and which was only used when the Doge went out on Ascension Day to 'marry the Adriatic' now no longer exists.

As you may imagine, with so much poverty there is no society. Instead therefore of having their houses open, the principal people have many of them a small room under the arcades of St. Mark, where they go to pass the evening, and where, at this season all the world assembles between the hours of ten and two in the morning; the day here is in fact completely turned into the night. It is easy to account for as the inhabitants naturally prefer the cool breezes of the evening to the broiling sun of the day. All their amusements therefore take place at night. I am disappointed in the theatre. I was in hopes to have met with a good set of actors who would have given some of the good pieces of Metastasio or Alfieri. But there is only one theatre open and in it they give nothing but operas which are not of the least use in teaching one the language. The ladies here frequent the coffee houses (which are never closed) as well as the men.

We have found here an Austrian General, commandant of the town, who has been most extremely kind to us both as a cicerone and as a host, for we have dined frequently with him. At present, of course, everything here is in their hands, and I fear even after the Congress of Vienna is likely to continue so. Nothing can be more unpopular than they are, and indeed nothing but independence will content the Venetians, particularly when they see their rival Republic, Genoa, re-established. They all ask us, 'Why did not you English come and take us under your protection, and then we were sure of freedom?' Most assuredly we ought to have done it, but we were ill-informed of the state of the French force in the town. I have sent you but a meagre, miserable account of this marvellous place, but the difficulties of description are great. I know not where to begin, or where to leave off!

We shall leave this place on Monday for Padua, where we will stay a day or two. We shall go from there by Verona to Mantua, whence I will again write to you. After that we make for Florence. They have all been very gay in London I see, in consequence of the arrival of the sovereigns. What amuses me most though, is that the people pay much more attention to Blücher than either the Emperor or the King of Prussia. He merits it, and I am only glad the people know how to distinguish. The Prince of Wales (although he must have had a thorn in his side) must be in his full glory with so many foreigners of distinction about him. I shall indeed be delighted to get to Florence, to meet with all your letters there. Had I only known we should have been so long on the road, I would have ordered them to be sent here, but Dumfries is in exactly the same scrape. Give my best love to my mother and Sarah. God bless you all. Your affectionate brother, Wm. Crackanthorpe."

Letter to Sarah.

"Florence, August 1st, 1814. My dear Sarah — I am sadly afraid that you may begin to be uneasy at not having heard from me for so long a time, but I really have had neither the means nor the opportunity of writing to you, so much have we been hurried for the last ten days. The

Florence in 1838

first moment, therefore, that I am able, I despatch this to you, to give you tidings of the lost sheep, and also a little intelligence which may not be altogether unacceptable either at Newbiggin or to my other northern friends.

We left Venice on the 11th and pursued our route through Verona, Mantua, and Bologna, all extremely interesting towns, as well from the remains of antiquity and the fine pictures which they contain as from the recent events, the country being in general the scene of the campaign. On all sides are fruit trees with vines twining round them and hanging in beautiful festoons, laden with grapes. From Bologna we then came to Florence, crossing the Appenines, a chain of mountains which may be

Elba

called the backbone of Italy. I was very much disappointed in them. I expected to find much more bold and magnificent hills. In some parts though the pass was very romantic, and in others it was so steep that for the first time in my life I had the satisfaction of travelling with oxen.

No sooner had we arrived at Florence — very late at night too — than we found our old friend Mr. Baillie, who had passed the winter at Vienna with us. He proposed to us to set out the next morning with a Mr. and Mrs. Orby Hunter to visit the Island of Elba. This was too tempting an offer to be refused, and accordingly we all packed off immediately for Leghorn. And here we had the good luck to meet with his Majesty's brig, the Charlotte, the captain of which most kindly offered to convey us over and bring us back to any point we liked.

After a most tranquil voyage, for it was calm almost the whole way, we anchored on the second day in the harbour of Porto Ferraio, and having fired a royal salute we went ashore, where with the greatest possible difficulty we procured ourselves a lodging. The next morning we paid our respects to General Bertrand, who, under the last dynasty was *Maréchal de la Cour*, a very distinguished military character, and who has followed his master in all his misfortunes, serving him with the greatest fidelity. He received us very politely, and having intimated to him our wish to be presented to the Emperor he told us he would take his Majesty's orders thereupon. No answer, however, was made to us that day, and our patience was quite exhausted when early next morning he came to us and told us that Buonaparte would receive us at nine in the evening, at the same time apologising to us for having kept us so long in suspense. Unfortunately we had carried over some unpleasant intelligence about an English frigate, the captain of which had been prevented from taking on board the mother who wished to pay her son a visit at Elba, and

Elba

Napoleon on Elba

who was hourly looked for. This was a great disappointment, and put Napoleon so out of humour that General Bertrand durst not put the question to him sooner about our presentation.

At the hour appointed we made our appearance at the Palace and were conducted by a chamberlain through a suite of rooms into the garden, which is upon the ramparts of the citadel overlooking the sea, where we were most courteously received by Buonaparte with Bertrand in waiting. He kept us about an hour in conversation, speaking generally upon indifferent subjects, but with a gaiety and gentlemanlike manner which quite astonished me. As we were all in uniform (which by the way I have no right to wear) he asked many questions about our militia, in all the details of which he appeared much better informed than any of us. He asked us whether we were not formed when he was at

Elba

Boulogne with his army, fearing an invasion, also how many years we served and how we were appointed. With Mrs. Orby he talked about the English manufactures which are made for ladies' dresses, and observed that she was not patriotic, as she wore a gown of French silk. He spoke with her of her family, and all this with an ease and good nature which I can assure you pleased us extremely. At intervals, though, he seemed to relapse into a kind of reverie, when his countenance wore an almost fiendish expression; the light of the moon shining on it perhaps increased and exaggerated it, and I doubt not that he breathed vengeance within himself against us for having dared to come and see him in his humility. Our audience, however, was most gracious, and although I only saw him as a wild beast in his cage, I nevertheless congratulate myself that I have been presented to the man who has made Europe tremble for so many years, and who nearly accomplished his scheme of universal domination. He still manifests the same restless disposition as ever, and has already begun to make great improvements which in the end will be extremely advantageous to the island, although the measures which he has taken are for the moment rather unpopular, cutting roads through the property of private individuals, raising eighteen months taxes in advance, converting a church into a theatre (which even in Italy they look upon as a profanation), building a *lazaretto*, which in so small a port will be of very little use, and raising a regiment, to put him in mind, I suppose, of his former power.

    He rises every morning at four, takes a ride to the country house which he bought since his arrival, the improvements of which he himself superintends, returns at eight to breakfast, occupies himself with his affairs (although I believe he neither writes nor reads a single word of any kind), then takes his siesta for a couple of hours, dines at five, and returns again in the

Elba

evening to his villa, where he stays sometimes till ten. Bertrand is almost his sole companion, and must begin, I think, to be horribly tired of his *séjour* at Elba. Buonaparte has 600 of the Old Guard with him, who volunteer to follow their master, and who are certainly the finest men I ever saw. They are now, though, I am told, beginning to be ennuyés, as they have nothing to do, and would be very glad to return. They call themselves, indeed, '*des esclaves'* and their officers *'des prisonniers.'* At the same time they speak most enthusiastically of the Emperor, and declare that nothing shall ever induce them to desert '*le grand capitaine'* in his misfortunes. He has also two mamelukes with him, and about forty Polish lancers, who attend him when he goes abroad. Nothing, though, can be more wretched than his equipages, for instead of all the fine carriages which we read in the newspapers of his having brought away with him, there are really none but the very refuse of his collection. His house, indeed, which is very small, is very neatly furnished, and he still keeps up (upon a reduced scale, of course,) all the pomp of a court with the same ceremony as at St. Cloud or Versailles. How different is all this from the conduct of Charles the Fifth, and how much more noble it would have been to have followed his example, and to have retired from the world, and to have prepared for his end, and, in fact, to have performed his own obsequies over himself like his illustrious predecessor. But no doubt he is, in spite of his great military genius, a man of a little mind ... Revengeful, obstinate, and cruel, he has brought upon himself his own ruin, and I cannot think but that many years will not pass over before his career will be completely finished.

After our interview we took our leave of the island and embarked again on board the Charlotte for the gulf of Spezia, which being in Genoese territory, made us escape the quarantine, an embargo imposed (as a political measure) in Tuscany upon all vessels coming from Elba. We arrived on the third day and proceeded through Lucca, so famous for its olives and its oil, to Florence, where we shall, I hope, stay some time, both to see its treasures and also the entrée of the Grand Duke. Your letters, I am sorry to say, have come by no means regularly. Charlotte's of the 14th of May is the last I have had. Most likely, however, they will all turn up at Rome, where Sligo, I presume, has sent them. The heat is excessive, but the evenings are so charming that I am willing to compound for passing the mornings shut up in the house that I may enjoy the breezes at night, when all the world is abroad to enjoy themselves. Already there is a colony of English established here, amongst them the Dashwoods who are pleasant people, but I cannot say much for the others … ever your affectionate brother, William Crackanthorpe."

Letter to Charlotte.

"September 4th, 1814.
As I have an opportunity of sending a letter to Vienna, whence I trust it will have a more certain conveyance than from the post here, I seize it, though it may be somewhat long on the road. I am now entirely alone, Dumfries having been called away to meet his family at Geneva. They are coming to pass the winter in Italy."

Dumfries's grandfather, Lord Bute, died in Geneva on 16th November 1814, and Dumfries (now 2nd Marquess of Bute) returned home.

"I can assure you I find a great loss in his departure, as I have rarely met with a man who possesses more good qualities or who promises more fairly to become a distinguished character … I have made considerable progress in Italian, but, unfortunately, even in Italy, opportunities are wanting to practise oneself in the tongue, for the little society into which one has the entrée is composed almost entirely of foreigners, and French is naturally the language spoken. The house I most frequent is that of the Countess d'Albany, a woman interesting from every point of view, and particularly so to an Englishman. The wife of the last Pretender to the crown of Great Britain, and now receiving a pension of £1,500 a year from us, the great friend of one of the most celebrated men that Italy has produced (I mean Alfieri, many of whose works she now possesses in MS.), a woman who knows and speaks all modern languages with the greatest fluency, and is well up in their literature as well cannot fail to be a companion of whom one would wish to make a friend. As for myself, I go to her house every evening, and nothing could be kinder than she is. She has opened her library to me, and given me leave to take what books I like. She has also about her a good many men of talent, and artists, who are, indeed, the only society which is to be found. As for the *noblesse,* it is really scandalous to witness the scenes of immorality on every side; no such thing as public opinion exists — the men are without any sense of honour, and the women without any principle, either of morality or religion … in this country, as Mr. Burke has said, we must live in retrospect, but how dreadful it is to think that the most beautiful, and, certainly, the most interesting country in the world should be inhabited by such a race! "

This censorious judgement sits uneasily beside Sligo's report to his mother on the 4th November, 1814. On his way to Rome from Florence he wrote, "I could no longer wait for Crackanthorpe who is in love and has gone on tour with his flame & her husband."

Nonetheless, Sligo himself could be shocked by the amorality he observed: he wrote to his mother on the 20th January 1814, "I am no prude but the commonest Brothel in London is not to be placed on any lower footing than many of the best houses here."

"Of politics I can tell you but little. The Austrians, however, have appropriated to themselves the whole of Lombardy, and it would appear that the poor Pope is to suffer to make a petty sovereignty for the Empress Marie-Louise. The idea now is that her destination is to be changed from Parma to Bologna, and that the ex-Queen of Etruria will be re-established in her right at Parma. If she had her rights she ought, I believe, to come here, for her father, the late King of Spain, actually bought Tuscany for her, but of this there is no probability, as the effects of the Grand Duke are actually arrived, and no doubt he intends to follow them shortly. Murat holds his kingdom by a very doubtful tenure; the Pope, I hear, has actually refused to acknowledge him, a refusal which I trust the allied Sovereigns will endorse.

Thus will Italy, unfortunately, instead of being united into one great Kingdom, by which means she might be raised into consequence, be broken up into twenty different little Governments, and thus lose again all the little spirit which the French had instilled into her, and become more degenerate than ever ... Sligo joins me in about a month's time. If he keeps his time we shall go together to Rome, if not I shall, I think, join the party of one of the daughters of the Prince de Ligne, who is going there with her husband. Colonel Campbell, the Commissary who is attached to Elba, has been here some days. He has told me many anecdotes of Buonaparte, which are extremely interesting. I may return to Elba for a day or two and I will then write you all in detail. The Grand Duke is expected on the 21st. We shall then have a series of fêtes, but all these things are horribly stupid when any branch of the House of Austria is concerned in them. Ahremburg waits for this letter as he has just determined to despatch a courier. My best love to my mother, your ever affectionate brother, William Crackanthorpe."

Florence

Letter to his mother.

"Florence, August 15th, 1814. My dear mother, — Just as I was on the point of writing to you, a packet of letters came to me from Rome — to my great joy — sent thither by Sligo. I must now endeavour to tell you somewhat of Florence and its society. It has not suffered like most of other places by the ravaging depredations of the French; the galleries are almost untouched, only the famous Venus has been taken. In the galleries I spend many hours daily to my infinite satisfaction. The Italian which is spoken here is the most pure — another inducement to remain. I daily feel myself improving and making steady progress.

In point of society, indeed, Florence, like all other parts of Italy, has little reason to boast. The inhabitants have no regard whatever to morality, there is no respect whatever paid to the marriage tie, the men are ignorant and debauched, and the women do not seem to have even the desire to please. It is impossible to associate with the higher classes, and one is obliged to seek the society of artists as the only companions, and delightful they are. Individually I have no reason to complain. Count Staremberg, now Governor of Tuscany, whose wife I knew at Vienna, has opened his house to me. His wife is a very charming woman, so I find their house a great resource. Then there is the Countess d'Albany, whom I mentioned in my last letter, the wife of the last Pretender. She is a woman of very remarkable talents, and she is in correspondence with all the *literati* of Europe. She is always at home from eight to ten, and I am always there between those hours.

Lord Dumfries has gone down to Rome, for being obliged to return home almost immediately he would not quit Italy without seeing Rome. I have preferred to wait until the unhealthy season there is over, and I shall meanwhile make some little excursions

Florence

in Tuscany. I begin by going to Lucca, to spend a few days there with the Starembergs, and I shall go on to Rome when I hear it is quite safe to do so. I am tolerably intimate with the Dashwoods, but of the rest of the English colony I know comparatively little, for I do not travel to meet my compatriots …

The Grand Duke is expected here shortly. His arrival is looked forward to with great anxiety, for it is then hoped that Tuscany will be disburdened of the load of German troops by which it is at present sorely oppressed. The Congress of Vienna will see all arrangements completed. I fear, however, that discontent will be the result, particularly if they are again submitted to Austria. Murat, too, will assuredly never be permitted to remain upon the throne of Naples, his conduct has been so treacherous to his benefactors. This letter goes *by post*, and so I know not whether I ought to write politics, but I will nevertheless venture it. My sisters have, I suppose, returned from their Yorkshire visit by now. I am forcibly reminded of Miss Sarah every morning when I find my buttons on the wrong side of my shirt. No doubt she is now making her usual havoc in the garden. Would I could transport her here where the hedges are of vine, the grapes hanging in tempting clusters on all sides. My best love to her and to Charlotte. — Your most affectionate son, Wm. Crackanthorpe."

Letter to Sarah.

"Florence, September 14th, 1814. My dear Sarah, — You see I am still here. I have remained much longer than I at first intended. First of all I wanted to see the arrival of the legitimate Sovereign. His entrée was all that could be desired, and he was received with the utmost enthusiasm. The Princes of the House of Lorraine are both merciful and kind to their subjects, and 3Tuscany—only a few short months ago a part

Florence

of the French empire—now no longer groans under the yoke of an oppressor. The conscription is abolished and peace is thoroughly established. I am much struck with the disposition of the Tuscans. They are a long-suffering, harmless people, the most amiable people possible, and, *amongst the lower orders,* extremely moral. If only a good example were set them by the noblesse, they would be the most virtuous people in the world. In the other provinces of Italy crime of all kinds (notably assassination) is but too common; here it is never heard of ... in fact, the lower classes are just as good subjects as the higher are bad.

The death of the Queen of Sicily (the mother-in-law of the Duke) has put a stop to all the fêtes which should have taken place. All the world is to put on black for a person no human being respects or regrets. Indeed, the horrors and cruelties of which this woman has been guilty exceed all belief. She was carried off by a stroke of apoplexy, without warning of any kind. All the English have been this morning to visit his Imperial Highness, and to offer their congratulations upon his return to his native country. Our reception was most gracious. Born, bred up, and educated here, it is not to be wondered at that he loves Tuscany, and as it has suffered the least of any country under French dominion, he has no heart-rending scenes to witness on his return. His palace, indeed, has been robbed of most of its best paintings. Sixty-three chefs d'oeuvre, amongst which were a dozen Raphaels, having been taken away to Paris, as well as the beautiful Venus de' Medici. I have really begun to know the galleries *en connaisseur* now. For the last few days I have had the pleasure of being cicerone to an old friend from Vienna, one of the daughters of the Prince de Ligne, who, with her husband, is making a little tour. With them I shall go up to Milan, on my way to meet Sligo, who is now in Switzerland. I have for the

Florence

present abandoned my plan to return to Elba. Colonel Campbell, with whom I should have gone, is here for the arrival of the Grand Duke, but I shall certainly hope to go when the opportunity offers.

The quantity of English here is prodigious; the bankers' books are full of names with letters of credit. Amongst them is the Princess of Wales. What *can* be her object in coming here? I trust not to play the fool with Lady Oxford at Naples (who was her great friend and is now the mistress of Murat). I begin to be very anxious with respect to the lot of this man. It is utterly impossible to admit him into the great family of Europe, for he is really a being unworthy of it. We are all looking forward eagerly to the arrival of Lord Burghersh, the minister here. What a delightful situation for a man who has any taste for art, and who knows how to live a rational life (which unfortunately those who preceded him did not). Everything, too, is so cheap that with only a moderate fortune a man may, comparatively, play the game of a Sovereign in comparison with what he could do on a like income in England. It is, indeed, one of the places I m most tempted to envy.

This evening we have an exhibition which is intended to imitate the Olympic Games of old. There will be a chariot race and the cars are modelled on those of ancient Rome. The Court will attend it and it will, no doubt, be a very pretty spectacle. There is also to be a race *without riders* which, I believe, is quite unique, and only to be seen in this country. It is amazing to see with what emulation the horses spurt on to the goal ...

Remember me to all my friends ... I am ashamed to send you so stupid a letter, but Florence is no place for news. Give my best love to my mother, who is at this instant perhaps in the old garden, and to Charlotte. Your most affectionate brother, William Crackanthorpe."

Milan

Corsa Venezia, Milan

Letter to his mother from Milan. October 10th, 1814.
"My dear mother, — You see I have made rather a retrograde movement by coming here from Florence instead of going straight to Rome. The fact is I heard that some of my Vienna friends were here, and amongst them particularly one of the daughters of the Prince de Ligne, and so I came.

This, evidently, was Flore, the youngest and reputedly the most intelligent of the daughters of the Prince de Ligne, gifted with an incisive wit resembling his, and wife since 1812 of Baron Spiegel, a Lutheran financier who was not considered an enlivening member of the Ligne circle. She was fifteen years older than William, but the frequent references to her suggest that she may have been the "flame" with whom, in Sligo's account, William had gone on tour. She had no children by her husband.

Milan

I also am very anxious to pass the Simplon, that most wonderful road which Buonaparte made across the Alps. It is, I understand, a masterpiece of engineering. Unfortunately the King of Sardinia has not the funds to keep it up, so that I fear in a very short time the avalanches will destroy it. Milan has more the air of a capital than any other great town upon the Continent I have yet seen. The movement in the principal streets is very considerable, and the number of splendid carriages which are to be seen daily on the Corso prove that the French whilst they were here did not rob universally. Buonaparte indeed has embellished the town considerably. He has finished the Cathedral, and has placed more than 1,300 marble statues in different niches about it. He also formed an academy for sculpture and painting, the galleries of which he has filled with some of the best modern paintings of Italy. Milan also was the residence of the Court – a most luxurious one – consequently the tradespeople were much enriched. Milan, therefore, from being the capital has now become a provincial town under the Government of Austria, which never was very famous for its encouragement either of useful or liberal institutions. Consequently thousands are discontented. They have lost their places and their pension, and an immense number of officers who were employed in the French army are actually starving from want. On all sides one hears nothing but murmurs of dissatisfaction and despair. If, however, some have lost, the majority have gained; their young men will no more perish on the plains of Spain or be frozen to death on the Moscow road. It is to be hoped that things will be placed on a peace establishment very shortly as the levies are terribly heavy still. The moment is indeed favourable for a most desirable revolution. Italy might now throw off the yoke of Austria, and establish herself as a great and independent kingdom. Once more she might perhaps see Rome, at present filled with monks and

Milan

priests, all equally ignorant and superstitious, a great capital and a centre of learning and civilization. However, I must leave these dreams; and now for its society. The leading feature in the character of Italians is the passion of avarice. To this feeling they sacrifice all their comfort, and their consequent demoralization is complete. Society, in its true sense, does not exist amongst them, as everyone is really too close to give his neighbour a dinner – nay, it goes even further, for, to spare the expense of a few wax candles, instead of holding their assemblies in their own private houses, they all go to the theatre (which in this country costs nothing), and in their boxes it is that they receive and pay all their visits. Far from going to the theatre to listen to the piece, a card table is introduced into one box and a supper into another; so that from eight in the evening till one in the morning the theatre is absolutely their reception room. And this is the life they lead from one year's end to another, dividing their time between their bed, their carriage, and the theatre.

Amongst the English travellers who daily arrive from England two more remarkable than the rest made their appearance yesterday; Catalani, the great singer, and The Princess of Wales. She (the latter) was at the play last night, and I understand the theatre is to be illuminated in her honour tonight. It will be a great sight, for the theatre is the finest in the world. She remains here about a fortnight, and then proceeds to Florence, Rome, and Naples, where her friend, Lady Oxford, has already taken a house for her. Never, in my opinion, was anything so ill-judged as this her journey; for as Buonaparte has taken all the pains possible to give every publicity to that unfortunate investigation"— (*instigated by the Prince Regent into his wife's supposed adulteries*) —"there is not one individual on the Continent who does not know the whole state of the case; and although everyone blames the Prince, it is naturally observed that

Milan

there must be some ground for the accusation. Morality indeed, it is true, is a word almost unknown here, and had she been guilty she would be readily excused. The questions, however, which they ask are sometimes very unpleasant, and most difficult to answer.

Lord and Lady Holland are also here, on their road further south. Florence, I should think, will have some unpleasant recollections for them ... Sligo has just sent me two Newbiggin letters from Florence, where he waits my return. We propose going together to Rome. I am, I flatter myself, become quite a *connoisseur* in the fine arts. Madame d'Albany gave me letters to some of the best artists here, and they have been of great service to me. Through my old friend Madame Spiegel I have obtained the entrée into almost all the best houses. I must confess that though they are perhaps not less ignorant than in the other towns of Italy, morality is more respected, and vice does not stalk about here in quite so barefaced a manner as elsewhere.

With respect to Kirkby Thore Common, I doubt not but that you have done the best. Your judgement in these affairs is better than mine. The proposed enclosure will indeed immensely improve the face of the country, and I trust that the proprietors will not neglect to plant a great part of it without delay. As to the climate here I can assure you it is quite as cold as at Newbiggin at this season, and as the houses are all built for summer you can have no idea how the cold makes itself felt – stone floors, without carpets, no chimney pieces, and single windows do not suit my views I can assure you. However I hope soon to move to a warmer atmosphere. I will not again talk of the fine climate of Italy, for we had snow in Florence on the 4th of September. I have just heard that the Princess of Wales is going to commit herself by giving a ball here. Remember me to all my friends. If I calculate right you will receive this about the time of the Penrith

Genoa

Porta della Lanterna, Genoa, 1818

races, where I trust you will enjoy yourself. My best love to my sisters. —Your most affectionate son, Wm. Crackanthorpe.

Letter to Sarah.

"Genoa, Oct. 2nd, 1814.
My dear Sarah, —I write to you with my windows open and the sun is hot as in the month of August in England. I arrived here two days ago. My stay in Milan was somewhat prolonged, and my tour to the lakes and afterwards to the top of the Simplon took me longer than I had anticipated. I was loth, too, to leave my good friends the Spiegels and so I lingered on. Nor indeed do I believe I should now have left it had I not fallen in with Lord and Lady B (*indecipherable*) two most delightful people, whom I meet with by accident on the top of the Alps. They were delayed by want of horses, and I had the good fortune to rescue them from

their embarrassment. I consequently joined them, and for the last fortnight we have been together, and here I have come with them. The Lago di Como is most beautiful and its scenery is greatly varied; in some places its banks have all the gaiety which art and nature can give them, in others they are stern, melancholy, and uninhabited. In general, though, the banks are most fully inhabited, and every village has its own peculiar trade or distinction. The one contains only fishermen, another boatbuilders, a third hewers of wood, whilst the inhabitants of others are vagabonds and wanderers over the whole face of Europe. All these people you meet with in England selling prints and barometers come from this place. Another village sends its men to Spain to seek their fortunes, and a third set will wend their way to Russia. In many parts also of the lake are to be seen the rich villas of the great Milanese nobles, upon whom, however, the beauties of nature appear to be quite lost, for they rarely pass more than two months of the year at them, as they cannot there enjoy the gossip of the city or idle away their time at the opera. Society indeed in Italy, I must repeat, is at its lowest ebb, and were it not for the artists and some foreigners who endeavour to make themselves agreeable I hardly know what one would do, so completely one would be obliged to live in the past. From the Lago di Como I passed over to the Lago Maggiore, which is immense, but the mountains surrounding it are not sufficiently high to relieve it, and it is therefore much less interesting than the other. From thence I proceeded through the famous Simplon Pass, made by Buonaparte - a marvellous performance of his truly, and one which would have daunted any spirit less enterprising than his own. (upon the top of this road it was that I met with my present companions, shivering amidst snows and surrounded by icicles.) I am glad indeed that I have seen this prodigious work. I then returned to Milan , and shortly afterwards

Genoa

I determined to come to Genoa by a new route. The whole of the country through which I passed is extremely interesting, as it was the scene of the Austro-Russian campaign at the beginning of the French Revolution. The town of Genoa stands on a bay only inferior to that of Naples. Its palaces are magnificent. They are collected together in two broad streets (the only ones into which carriages can be admitted.) They produce an effect of the magnificence and wealth of the town in its old days. Like all the other ports on the continent, however, Genoa has suffered under the tyranny of Buonaparte, and although now that it is under English protection trade has begun to revive, it can never again, I imagine, rise to its former wealth and splendour. Its fate is indeed at present very uncertain, and they are all here waiting most anxiously to learn the result of the deliberation of the congress, as they will then know whether it is to be restored as a Republic or merely to be declared a free town. For the moment indeed it is garrisoned by British troops, and I can easily imagine myself to be in England when I see out of my window a fleet of our men of war in the harbour and red uniforms parading all the streets. The commandant, Sir John Dalrymple, has been extremely kind to us, and I think we shall remain here a little longer. We shall, I am sorry to say, have to part company, for Lord B- is obliged to go home, whilst I shall return to Florence, where Sligo is waiting for me to go on to Rome.

The Princess of Wales has been playing the most foolish card possible. So bad, indeed has been her conduct at Milan, and so improperly did she choose her company, that even Italians were shocked and indignant (imagine, therefore, what it was). All the world excuses the Prince, and the English do all in their power to avoid her, so ashamed are they of her Royal Highness's behaviour. Of political news I can send you no details. 'On dit', that Murat is to be left upon the throne of Naples, no preparations

Florence

as yet having been made for turning him out. ... How I wish that you had at Newbiggin the climate we are now enjoying. My mother would then have no stiff necks ... God bless and preserve you, your affectionate brother, Wm. Crackanthorpe. "

Letter to his mother.
"Florence, October 17th, 1814. Dear Mother - Here I am again returned to Florence! I had a most delightful tour in Lombardy. Genoa, as a city, has perhaps struck me more than any other place on the Continent that I have yet visited. Its palaces, its harbour, its streets are all alike splendid. The coup d'oeil it presents is indeed unique. It is a place too frequently passed over by English people, and I congratulate myself that I have seen it ... As there is no road from Genoa to Florence I was obliged to embark on the gulf of Spezzia ... and Sir John Dalrymple, who is there in command, was kind enough to give me a passage on board a transport which he ordered round there for me. The spot where I embarked, the little town of Lerici, is one of the most beautiful places I ever saw, both by land and sea its position is unrivalled, the necessaries of life are to be had in the greatest abundance ... On my way I visited Carrara, the home of the finest and purest marble, and saw the immense establishment there for young men to come and study the art of sculpture. Here indeed 'the pregnant quarry teems with human form,' as there is there scarcely any fine ancient model which one does not find copied. The modern works, too, are some of them extremely good. I must allow in fairness to the French Government that it did all in its power to encourage the arts, and it is quite astonishing how many immense groups are now even in hand for the different buildings which Buonaparte was going to adorn had he remained on the throne. Since his fall the artists

Florence

are quite in despair, for private individuals in this country are far too close and parsimonious to think of employing them, and the people of all other countries except our own are much too poor. Upon the English, therefore, they rely entirely, and I trust, poor people, that they will not be disappointed. I stayed two days at Lucca with Count Stahremberg, who is Governor there, and whose wife I had known at Vienna, and they were as kind as ever. Florence at this moment is much more like an English than an Italian town in point of society. All the inns are completely full, the galleries are crowded, and one sees nothing but little bonnets and long coats instead of French fashions. I must say that the contrast between the dress of our own country women and that of the natives is really extremely striking, and I must further confess that the advantage is not on our side! In the evening this is particularly to be remarked, for so short and scanty are their petticoats and really so indecently are they exposed that even Italians are shocked ... Immense numbers are gone to Rome and Naples for the winter... On Saturday I shall set out for this once mistress of the world. I shall sleep the first night at Sienna and then go straight on. Directly I arrive I shall write to you at once and I only wish that I had the wings of a dove to avoid the rascality of the post masters, inn keepers and postilions; one has to bargain for everything ... The Princess of Wales, has, I understand, most unthinkingly gone on to Naples, so that she, in her high situation, has done what even private individuals thought imprudent and incautious ... Indeed, on one occasion, she thus expressed herself, 'I am not English, I am German,' meaning by that, I suppose, to palliate her conduct and excuse her indiscretions. We are all heartily ashamed of her, and regret extremely that she has come on the Continent.

I can send you no news of the Congress, Affairs, though, I fancy go pretty well, and we shall certainly at length have a

Rome

Rome: View of the Colosseum by J Smith

peace. I fear it may not be a very durable one. The ambition of Russia is too unbounded, the faith of Austria is too proverbial, and the restlessness of France too evident to allow of things remaining long tranquil. It is very certain that the people of every country are tired of war and long for peace. The season is now delightful, but the weather has been most uncertain. Immense quantities of rain have fallen, rendering travelling in Lombardy most unpleasant. The sun today is exquisite. Remember me to all my friends in the north ... Has Colonel Salkeld yet bought Acorn Bank? In this case we shall have him for a permanent neighbour. - Your ever affectionate son, Wm. Crackanthorpe."

The Congress of Vienna opened on 1st November, 1814. Letter to Charlotte.

Rome

"Rome, December 1st, 1814. My dear Charlotte, At length I am arrived in this most interesting city. I was long in coming, but I am not sorry for the delay, as the season is now neither too cold nor too hot, and I can be abroad the whole day looking at the wonders and curiosities with which it is filled. The road from Sienna passes through the most beautiful country in the world. I fear the north, however great its moral advantages, cannot compare with it! The contrast as we approached Rome was indeed striking. For the distance of twenty miles, indeed from the moment that the cupola of St. Peter's came into sight, not a cottage nor an habitation is to be seen. The whole country is totally abandoned, the ravaging hand of a deadly plague seems to have swept everything away, and nothing but barren wastes extend themselves before you. As soon as we entered the gate we seemed to perceive the phantom of ancient Rome that awaited us; the ghost of its former majesty seemed to be stalking the streets and haunting us amongst ruined churches and neglected palaces. It appeared to conduct us to a most miserable inn and there take up its abode with us! The melancholy and saddening appearance of this town exceeds all belief. A general gloom lies over all, and the old equipages one meets in the streets carry one back to the fourteenth century. If in general Rome may be called gloomy, in detail it is most magnificent. St. Peter's is beyond the powers of all human imagination to describe. The exterior, perhaps, is not so striking as St. Paul's, inasmuch as the Vatican being about it detracts from its proportional grandeur, but the interior, how shall I attempt to give you an idea of it! Here it would appear that architecture, sculpture, and painting have all been carried to the greatest perfection, and that here exists the proudest monument of human ingenuity ...

In the centre of the section of the cross lies, in a vault, the body of the great Apostle; around it is a balustrade upon which are placed 112 lamps, which are kept perpetually burning, and at no time of the day can one enter without seeing hundreds of people on their knees around it, counting their rosaries. Immediately behind it is the great altar, standing perfectly isolated and raised seven steps above the floor. This altar is decorated by a magnificent canopy, supported by four spiral columns, all of bronze. The height of this canopy is 124 feet, and it cost in its manufacture alone (the metal itself being all robbed from the Parthenon) the enormous sum of £30,000. It is, however, quite impossible to me to give you any true idea of St. Peter's ... . Let me recommend you to read Eustace's Tour in Italy. It will give you a better idea of Rome and the country than any book I know. It will be a pleasure to me to think that whilst you are examining Rome on paper I am treading among its actual ruins, and that we are thus both employed in similar occupations ... As for myself I have begun to see Rome with a cicerone. It is better, I think, at first to have everything worthy of notice pointed out to you, and then afterwards make your own way about alone. I have therefore begun with ancient Rome. I am oftentimes obliged to call in the aid of fancy, and this morning I was actually obliged to transform a cow into Cicero, as it was just occupying the place where the rostrum in the forum stood! Lamentable are the debris on all sides. Perhaps a single column is all that remains of the finest temple - on all sides arches are either tottering or actually fallen, whilst some have been allowed to become buried in the earth about them. Of modern Rome I have as yet little or no idea. For travellers it has lost much of its interest, as so many of its best collections of both pictures and statues have been stolen and transported to Paris by Buonaparte. Much, however, remains ...

Of society also I yet know nothing. The Princess Czartoryska, to whom were my best letters of introduction, has

Rome

been ill ever since I came, and I have seen very few other people. Here, perhaps, society is less necessary than in any other place. The morning is occupied in seeing sights, the evenings I pass in reading the history of the arts, and thus preparing myself for my next morning's enjoyment ... Of the politics of this part of the continent, we yet know nothing. Everything with respect to Murat is kept a profound secret, and there is no doubt but that you in England will know his fate long before we do. I am told that he has treated all the English who have gone down there with the most marked respect, and whatever may be the determination of the allies he holds himself ready to meet his fate with firmness and intrepidity. The poor Pope is doing everything in his power to relieve his people of their burden. He sacrifices nearly all his revenues to ameliorate their lot, and from all I hear he appears to be a most excellent man. I presume I shall have the honour of kissing his toe some day ere long, of which I will write you a detailed account! Sligo has gone on to Naples, as he could not bear the stupidity of the place, there being no society nor theatre where he could pass his evenings. I shall follow him in a fortnight for the Carnival, and return here for the Holy Week. There is so much to see that I think I shall never get through ... God bless and preserve you all. - Your most affectionate brother, Wm. Crackanthorpe."

Letter to Charlotte.

Rome, December 12th, 1814.
"My dear Charlotte - I received your letter with delight yesterday, for in it you give me a great consolation. You tell me you hear regularly from me! So ill are the posts managed in this country that I am in perpetual fear that you may be uneasy about me ...

Rome is one of those places which the more one sees of it the more one is delighted and astonished. It is three weeks since

Rome

I arrived. I have not lost one single morning and yet I have not got through half of its curiosities. Every private house is still more or less rich in statues, pictures, or antiques. Happy those who saw Rome before the French entered it, for since that time it has of course lost many of its chefs d'oeuvre. Eighty of them were indeed stipulated to be given up by treaty, as if the object of war was solely plunder and robbery! Then too the enormous contributions which have since been levied on the town have forced private individuals to sell some of their greatest art treasures at very inferior prices. Consequently many of the villas, a kind of 'maison de plaisance' which the Roman nobles possess just without the walls of the town, and to which they go to breathe a little fresh air in the summer - houses fitted up with a luxury of which we in England have no idea, are completely spoliated and ruined. This very morning I have been to view what was considered the most beautiful of the kind in Rome; the walls are all encrusted with fine marbles, the vaults of the rooms painted by the best masters, columns of porphyry or 'verde antique' supported the doors, the finest Greek statues filled the niches ... At present this 'specimen palace' is in a state of utter desolation. The gilded ornaments, it is true, remain, but all the antique statues are gone, their places filled with plaister figures. The rich marbles have all been sold, and the proprietor, no longer able to bear the sight of it, allows it to fall of itself into a mass of ruin and destruction. This is not a solitary instance, on all sides the ravaging hand of French plunderers shows itself too plainly by the ruin of palaces, churches and convents.

    I took yesterday the round which is, I think, the most interesting in all Rome. I will give you a little sketch of it, and you can then imagine my delight. Setting out from the Capitol, I traversed the Forum. Here imagination is obliged to do all, for this most famous spot is now converted into a cattle market. From

Rome

the Forum I proceeded to visit the baths of Caracalla. The ruins of these baths are enormous, and give one a just idea of the luxury and magnificence of that age. I then went on to visit the tombs of the Scipios. This is a discovery which has only been made within a few years ... Hence I passed by the tomb of Horatio, imagining to myself the while Rome as she was ... Pursuing then the Appian Way, which now remains just as when it was first made, its sides adorned with different tombs now mouldering into dust and covered with ivy, I came to the circus of Caracalla. Here the chariot races took place, here the Roman people came to be amused by the national games. Afterwards, turning homeward, I passed by the grotto of Egeria, still bearing the marks as described by Ovid, where Numa used to come and hold converse with this mysterious nymph. And so I pass every day! Turn on which side of Rome you will, the imagination is ever nourished, the eye ever delighted. To St. Peter's I always go last, for here all the gloomy and melancholy reflections ... vanish ... and here I close each day.

The English colony seems to increase every hour. With the greatest difficulty do the newly-arrived find a place in which to lay their heads. After Christmas, though, many will push on to Naples, and though the society is as well composed in general as it can be, I shall nevertheless not be at all sorry for it. As for the Romans, they are no resource at all. They rarely open their houses, either from poverty or from their jealousy of foreigners. Were it not that there are a few Polish families in the city we should be almost without society. The Romans, too, are extremely ignorant. Of literature they know nothing, and even in the politics of their own country they appear to take little interest. The Pope I have not yet been presented to; I am, I believe, to pay him a visit next week. He is a fine, venerable old man, but much more calculated to govern spiritual than temporal things. After

Rome

seeing his Holiness, I shall in all probability see the Queen of Etruria, who, from her misfortunes and sufferings under the last dynasty of France, must be a most interesting person. Rome, indeed, appears to be the retreat of all the abdicated or chasséd sovereigns. At present it contains a legitimate King of Spain, of Sardinia, and Etruria, besides I know not how many others, and Buonaparte's brothers, who have all played their part in the puppet show.

The snow is not, I hope, so deep but that you can get to Acorn Bank and Temple Sowerby to see your neighbours ... I am delighted with the account you give of my mother, who you say is as blooming as ever. My best love to her and to Sarah.-Your ever affectionate brother, Wm. Crackanthorpe.

I have latterly made considerable progress in Italian. I now begin to explain myself without much difficulty; but no one must imagine that he can speak Italian because he can read it fluently, the language of the books being so different from that of familiar conversation. The climate here is divine; the sun has as much power as in October at Newbiggin, and, as almost all the trees are evergreens, the winter is scarcely perceived at all."

Letter to his mother.

"Rome, January 7th, 1815. My dear mother, - I have just this instant had a letter from Sarah, which I can assure you has caused me no small degree of uneasiness, inasmuch as it so strongly urges my return to England , upon the grounds of your apprehension for me and depression of spirits. This, I am sure, would be a sufficient reason for my setting out immediately did I not conceive that there are inducements to make me prolong my stay at present, which upon further consideration I doubt not but that you will find abundantly convincing to make a somewhat further sacrifice, and to permit

Rome

me to defer my return home for a few months longer. The very great uncertainty that I shall ever again have the opportunity of visiting the Continent makes me wish to profit by the present. I am arrived at that age when I can enjoy everything the most, and I trust my time is not altogether lost. The seeds of a future war are now sowing at the Congress; Europe will not improbably undergo another revolution, and the hostile spirit in France is, I understand increasing daily. All these things, which, in my opinion, are more than probabilities, may suddenly close, and put an end to the intercourse which now subsists between England and the other European powers. We may again be shut up as we have been for the last twenty years ... Italy, too, is not a country to be hurriedly visited ... It brings back freshly the history of the last twenty-five hundred years ... At present also a great revolution is here at work. The people are at last beginning to feel the degraded state in which thy have been for ages past imperceptibly gliding. The effects of the old system which the French abolished and the new one which they introduced are now acting in collision the one against the other, and a great good must clearly be the consequence. The nation, in fact, is in the commencement of regeneration ... Independence is now the universal cry, liberty and freedom the two blessings which the people earnestly wish for. By a cursory visit therefore it is not possible to form any opinion of the state of Italy, and I am fully persuaded that to enter fully into its past as well as its present one must dwell in the country some time, learn its language, read its councils, and seek information on all sides. These are the reasons which have detained me here so long, and I trust you will see their weight, and will make no objections to my further remaining until the end of the month of March. I fix this time for I desire to pass the Holy Week at Rome, and to have sufficiently long interval between now and that time in which to visit Naples

Rome

which, as you may conceive, must be extremely interesting. Switzerland too will then be visitable, the snow will have melted and the spring begun. This then is my present plan. I am willing to abandon it should you make any objections, and I will come home through France immediately. At the same time I must express to you how great would be my regret at leaving Italy before I had thoroughly seen it. May I therefore ask you to make this sacrifice in addition to the many others you have already made on my account, and I trust that I have not altogether failed in shewing you sufficient reason why I am induced to make this request.

Since I last wrote I have assisted at High Mass sung by the Pope. His Holiness does this three times a year at the great altar in St. Peter's. I cannot say that as a religious ceremony it is very striking, for the splendour and magnificence of a temporal prince do not at all accord with the simplicity of our ideas of religion. I must confess that it appeared to me much more like a Lord Mayor's procession than an humble service offered to the Creator. Our Gothic cathedrals, too, are much more suited for such solemn services than St. Peter's. No pealing organs are permitted to sound the note of praise, and a few voices, however fine they may individually be, are completely lost in the immensity of this mighty pile. Nor did there appear to be any feeling of devotion in the audience. The cardinals were arraying their robes, the prelates officiously attending to the Pope's petticoats, the people staring about them, and the only one who seemed to enter into the true spirit of the ceremony was his Holiness himself. There is one moment which is, I must confess, very striking, and that is when, upon the elevation of the Host, the whole multitude in one instant fall on their knees. They seem to be really inspired with the awe of the real presence, and, a dead silence prevailing, the effect is very imposing. I am just this

Rome

moment come from an audience with the Pope, and instead of kissing his toe have had the honour of kissing his hand. He is a very affable, pleasant, and agreeable old man, and, if one may judge from his countenance, has all the virtues. In the course of his conversation (which was not very interesting) he gave us a short sketch of the sufferings he underwent when a prisoner at Fontainebleau. One is only astonished that he has survived so long and terrible an imprisonment. He seems, however, better fitted for a spiritual than a temporal prince, for in affairs of government he is wholly guided by men as ignorant as he is himself, and although burdens have been lightened since his return, old customs still remain in use which are an actual disgrace to humanity, and which in civilized countries would not be permitted. He is himself a good and pious old man, earnest in his desire to do good, and most exemplary in his private life; but he has not the qualities of a great sovereign. How, indeed, could it be expected that he should have?

I have just had letters from Vienna announcing to me the death of my kind old friend the Prince de Ligne. It was in his house that I passed all my evenings, and to him I owe the chief part of my pleasure at Vienna. With wit, good breeding, and unrivalled powers of repartee, he was in addition the most delightful companion I ever knew, and the kindest friend. His house was open to everybody, and the best society was always to be met at it. His family are all in despair, for although they must have expected the event, he was the great keystone which kept them all together, and the centre to which they all clung ...

We are all anxious to know what passes at the Congress, and great anxiety is felt as to the dominions of the Pope, for, if they do not give him back the Marché of Ancona, I do not know how he is to support his Papal dynasty. It is said that his Holiness has threatened to use his spiritual arms, and that he will freely excommunicate any Catholic powers who are parties to his spoliation! But in these days the Church has not the power it once had, when Emperors had to come and sue for pardon barefoot.

The letter which Sarah mentions about Lancaster's farm has never come to hand, and therefore I beg you will act precisely as if I had nothing to do in the matter, for your judgement will be right. The English colony increases daily; not a single lodging is now to be had in this great town. Amongst the last arrived are the Duke and Duchess of Bedford with their niece. She will, I fear, never leave Rome, the state of her health is so bad. My best love and many happy new years to you all. Your affectionate son, Wm. Crackanthorpe."

Letter to Sarah.

"Rome, Jan.18th, 1815.

My dearest Sarah, - So shameful has been the derangement of his Holiness's posts that I really do not know whether my last letters have reached you or not. I am therefore determined to profit by a conveyance which the French Ambassador has established between this place and Paris, which prevents letters being detained, opened, and read at Turin. My last letter has, I trust, been satisfactory in giving my mother the reasons why I desire to prolong my stay in Italy. I could not have seen Rome in less time than that I have actually given. As it is, I shall, I know, depart before I have seen nearly all of its wonders and sights. I think the method I have adopted is a satisfactory one, for I began by taking the antiquities chronologically - working through the remains of the buildings of the ancient kings up to the Consular age, and at last to the time of Augustus, when the arts had reached their utmost pitch of perfection. Thus far my task was delightful enough, but then followed what is ever melancholy and disagreeable. I mean the tracing their decline and fall to the lower ages of the Empire, when architecture no longer pleases the eye with the justness of its proportions, and sculpture loses all the grace and spirit of its form. It was during the Medicean era that Rome, drawing wealth into its coffers from all corners of the world, shone forth in all her splendour, and stupendous indeed are the monuments left to us by that time ... The tide, alas, has again gradually ebbed until our own days. I think I may say I see signs that its reflux has commenced - particularly in the art of sculpture. There are two artists here, who, if not equal to those of ancient Greece, are certainly the best since Michael Angelo. The one a Dane, Thorwaldsen by name, famous for his 'basso relievos', the other an Italian, called Canova, famous for his statues. I believe that if the affairs of Europe were only settled we should soon have abundant proof that art still lives. How delightful this occupation of tracing undulations in the progress and decline of the arts is I could hardly indeed tell you. I only wish I could transplant you here to share it with me.

This day week begins the Carnival at Rome. It lasts, I believe, eight days. At its close I shall immediately set out for Naples. Many of the English colony have already gone there, particularly those who are anxious to secure good lodgings, which are very difficult to obtain. I am greatly looking forward to my stay there, for nothing can be more interesting than to observe a new Government and the effect it produces on the people. I cannot help wishing that Murat may, after all, be confirmed there, as I am confident that Naples will be infinitely better governed under him than under any Bourbon. Indeed there does not seem to be any sign of turning him out; our English fleet is withdrawn from the Mediterranean, and the Austrians have no army in Italy. These things make me think that all will remain quiet, which heaven grant, for we have been sufficiently tormented with war. How happy I am to see to-day that we have

Naples

at length made peace with America - at least then England is to enjoy a time of peace and tranquillity! At Vienna no progress appears to be making, and if you could only see the anxiety with which people look forward to their fate you would most heartily pity them. Indeed it is no exaggeration to say that all those countries such as thee major part of Italy , which have had the misfortune of being governed by Provisional Governments, are almost entirely ruined. Contribution has followed contribution. The commanding officers have burdened them with extraordinary requisitions (for their own pockets), and the soldier never hesitates to commit any outrage, imagining himself to be in an enemy's country. Discontent is everywhere, and aggravated misery on all sides. The picture of the Marché of Ancona is truly deplorable, for everything is eaten up either by the rapacity of the Government, the avarice of the Generals, or the lawlessness of the soldiery. The rich are ruined, the poor starving. I wish, therefore, that ministers would look at and attend to this state of things rather than think of amusing themselves with fetes and balls - these appear to be their present occupations."

This echoes the celebrated remark of the Prince de Ligne — "*Le congrès ne marche pas. Il danse*".

I must now beg you to remember me to my friends in the north, who have survived the dreadful storm with which you have been assailed. God preserve you all
. Your affectionate brother, Wm. Crackanthorpe."

Letter to his mother.

"Naples, Feb. 10th, 1815. My dear Mother, - I am at length got down to Naples. I had two delightful months at Rome, for, Athens excepted, it is the most interesting city in the world. To me it is one of the most melancholy places imaginable, and so striking is the contrast

General View of Naples by Weisbeck, 1835

between it and Naples that I do not at present feel reconciled to the change. In the one the streets are totally depopulated, in the other more crowded than the Strand in London; at Rome desolation and wretchedness are the striking features; bustle and noise are those of Naples. In point of locale Naples remains unsurpassed. I had heard much, but what I have seen surpasses far my anticipations. On getting here I felt for the first time the real advantages of a southern climate. At Terracini, about half way between Rome and Naples, the effects of the sun first show themselves. Here for the first time one meets with groves of orange trees, which in this month of February are in full bloom and bearing. Aloes and palms in the open air, narcissus and jonquil growing wild and in flower, the hedges filled with sweet

Naples

smelling plants, summer in fact everywhere. In this natural paradise, as it were, where the climate in winter is never cold, nor in summer too hot, from the continual sea breezes, lies the town of Naples, the third most populous city in Europe, for it boasts 500,000 inhabitants. With all its natural advantages it is, in all other respects, inferior, for its people are without any principle whatever, whether moral or religious. Poverty appears in every shape, and liberty and independence are utterly unknown. Much, though, has been done in these later years; a race of people called lazzaroni, who, having no place to lay their heads save the street, and numbering some 30,000, have been almost annihilated. The people are just beginning to feel their consequence as a nation, and the new system of laws which has been given them is only inferior to our own. As soldiers, too, they have given convincing proof of their courage, and a finer army, amounting to 80,000 men, I never saw. The present King is ready to meet the decisions of the Congress, whatever they may be.

To-morrow is appointed for our presentation at Court. Everyone is in raptures with the manners of the King and the way in which the English are received here is quite delightful. Some indeed have doubted upon the propriety of going to Court before the English Government have acknowledged the King and sent a minister here. I think, however, that if one enters his dominions that is a most perfect acknowledgment, seeing that one travels under his passport protected by his police; and so thinking of him as the first magistrate, I can conceive no objection to go and see him ...

The Princess of Wales, has, as you know, been here more than three months, and it is uncertain how much longer she remains. She is, of course, extremely civil to all the English, and has her house open twice a week, when all may go who have been presented to her. She also gives perpetual dinners. I have

Naples

already dined there twice besides having accompanied her up Vesuvius. This was, as you may imagine, no light labour, as she had to be carried up upon mens' shoulders the whole way, and the ascent is extremely sharp. However, she accomplished it! Luckily, upon her arrival at the mouth of the crater it fired a royal salute, making a great explosion and sending forth a shower of hot stones which fell all around us. The perpetual noise caused by the steam coming out of the fissures is quite tremendous and the columns of fire and smoke constantly arising give one a wonderful idea of the vastness of nature's operations. That the ancients should have thought it the entrance to the infernal regions is not to be wondered at. The expedition answered all our expectations, and the day went off very agreeably. The Princess though, I must add, is I fear going on but very indifferently. She forgets her dignity, talks upon the most serious subjects with the most astonishing indifference, and by no means conducts herself either to gain the respect of foreigners, or, with all her undoubted good nature, the regard of her compatriots. I cannot, though, be more explicit at present."

Sligo, however, could be much more explicit in his correspondence with his friend Lord Lowther, one of the Prince of Wales's circle of supporters to whom he was sending intimate reports of the Princess's behaviour. He had earlier written from Naples that "Crackenthorpe who as you know is a great friend wrote from Milan that even there people were so shocked that they had resolved to cut her (the princess) entirely." *Sligo added,* "I don't know who is rogering the Princess now but I will try to find out."

Sligo and William met again in Rome and returned to Naples from where Sligo resumed his correspondence to Lowther. "I have been making some enquiries from a courier of mine, a very clever fellow ... he began joking about the Princess's courier

... a fellow of 6 foot 3 inches & remarkably handsome who suddenly appeared very rich ... in short I think it very likely that he does the job for her ... I have been enquiring if he goes to the bawdy house & find that he never does now." This was apparently the early stage of the Princess's relationship with Bartolomeo Pergami cited in later proceedings in the House of Lords as *'a licentious, disgraceful and adulterous intercourse,'* demanding that the marriage between Caroline and the King (as the Regent had by then become) be *'wholly dissolved, annulled, and made void.'*

Sligo at this time seems to have hoped that his services as informer might lead to an appointment in Naples, where he now wished to remain. Soon afterwards, however, he was recalled to London by a crisis in his mother's marriage to the judge Sir William Scott, brother of Lord Chancellor Eldon. *"My mother's ménage is going on infamously ill,"* he wrote to Lowther, *"I fear that the old couple having committed the folly of being joined will commit the still greater one of separating afterwards."*

William resumed to his mother -

"I have seen very little of the society of this place, as the Court has been absent these few days at a chasse in the country. I am told though that I shall presently find many agreeable people. At present the only person I have seen is a Princess Castel Franco, a sister of Madame d'Albany. She is a very pleasant and well informed person, but as she is of the Anti-Court party, she rarely goes out.

Did you receive - I trust you did - my letter from Rome, in which I stated my reasons for wishing to prolong my stay abroad. I know not when such an opportunity may occur again ... This goes by a private hand - Heaven knows whether it will ever reach you. All the posts in Italy are stopped and for nearly a month we have had no letters. I must repeat that I beg you will not be

Naples

uneasy if you do not hear regularly, for the difficulty of finding opportunities of sending letters is great. My best love to my sisters. - Your affectionate son, Wm. Crackanthorpe.

On 26th February Napoleon left Elba, and on March 1st he arrived in France.

Naples, March 3rd, 1815.

My dearest Mother, - It is now more than two months that we have had no letters owing to some misunderstanding with the King of Sardinia about the postal arrangements. I am, as you can conceive, extremely uneasy on two accounts, first that you do not receive my letters, and that you may therefore be unhappy about me, and secondly that I have no intelligence from you to inform me how you are and what you are doing. I lose no opportunity of writing, but as all letters now go by private persons the opportunity of sending them comes but seldom.

I went to Pompeii, an ancient Roman town, which seventeen hundred years ago was completely covered by a shower of ashes and cinders after one of the most dreadful eruptions of Vesuvius. It is situated at five or six miles from the crater and yet so completely was it covered in every part that the situation of the town was totally imperceptible. By mere accident about 70 years ago, some traces of it were found; this led to further search, and at present, by the continued excavations, whole streets are laid open exactly as they were two thousand years ago. The internal economy of those times may thus be traced in very detail, the shops of the baker and the vintner are thrown open with all their different utensils, the various temples with their statues and other insignia of Pagan rites may be seen unaltered and intact. The Forum, with its bench of justice, is complete, except that having suffered a few years ago from an earthquake the columns which were then shaken are not yet quite

Naples

repaired. In fact an ancient Roman town, with skeletons for inhabitants only, may be seen in perfect integrity. Perhaps the most interesting part is the street which conducts to one of the gates, and which was used as a general burying place. There are all the different tombs (some of them most magnificent) arrayed in a double row. I entered the town this way, and I could not help thinking of the story in the Arabian Nights, of someone going into a city where he found everything converted into stone and everything without sound or motion. By the same eruption the town of Herculaneum was destroyed. Many interesting discoveries have been made there too, which have cleared up many doubts and explained to us the precise manner in which the ancients built their houses, arranged their theatres, and managed their domestic concerns.

The country to the west of the town is full of interest, as here lies all the scenery which Virgil has so happily described, and which still bears the same character which he has given it. At length one passes by his tomb, and laments over the ingratitude of men which has permitted it to fall to ruins. In a few years' time perhaps it may be hardly distinguishable.

Since I last wrote to you I have been twice or thrice to Court. Nothing can be kinder than the manners of the King and Queen, and although the etiquette is excessive, nevertheless it is as little formal as possible, owing to the gracious manner in which we English in particular are treated. No one knows whether the King is to remain or not. He is, however, fully prepared for all chances. He has a magnificent army of 85,000 men with which to defend himself if needs be. With them, he is, I hear, very popular, and I doubt not they will fight for him to the last.

<u>A rumour is abroad that Buonaparte has left Elba and is gone to France in</u> pursuit of his high destinies. You must not, however, be under any apprehension, as we are as safe here under the

King's protection as in any other spot. We must wait a little time to see what turn affairs take, and then turn our faces home as quickly as possible - be perfectly easy, for indeed we are in the best place possible."

This was a delusion due to the Neapolitan Governments' policy of secrecy. In fact, Naples declared a war of 'Italian Independence' on 15th March and launched an offensive against Austrian forces in Italy.

"Sligo takes this letter, as he is going home immediately, travelling day and night in consequence of the probable separation between his mother and Sir William Scott. I could wish him to stay a few days longer to see how things go, but he cannot be persuaded. I shall go to Rome for the Holy Week, and thence to Milan and Genoa, on my road to England. Still send your letters to Sligo and he will, when he gets to London, forward them on to me. The Princess of Wales still remains here, and seems uncertain about her departure; the sooner she goes the better. My best love to Charlotte and Sarah. - Your ever affectionate son, Wm. Crackanthorpe."

On March 20th Napoleon entered Paris and took power. On the 25th the Seventh Coalition was formed in Vienna.

"Rome, April 4th, 1815.

My dear Mother, - I find at this instant General Chowne passing through on his way to England; but, as he does not stay one moment, being on his road from Naples, I have only time to add that I am still here awaiting the advance of the Neapolitan troops yet a little nearer before I set out. I shall then make immediately for Florence, and then come through Germany. Rome is perfectly quiet. The Pope, it is true, is gone, and there is no Government, but all wears a most solemn appearance. Do not fear for my safety; the most respectable part of the colony still

Rome

remains - the Duke of Bedford's family and Lady Holland's, besides many others. We all remain till we know something certain, and then, I suppose, we shall take flight for Germany.

Of news we know nothing, save that in France things have gone as ill as possible. Murat, I imagine, if he finds himself strong enough, will declare himself King of Italy, and then a war with Austria will be inevitable. We have nothing to fear, but I am very anxious to know what part England will take - not, I hope, the one of embarking on a new war after 25 years of such dreadful convulsions. I cannot too often repeat, have no fears for me. Let the worst come to the worst, I can always get to the sea, and then embark for Trieste, going from there through Germany, and keeping to the rear of the armies. The spring is delightful; Rome is in its fullest beauty; but the horses are at the door, and I must write no more. Forgive this scrawl. God bless you and preserve you from all fears, as I am as safe as in England. -Your ever affectionate son, Wm. Crackanthorpe. "

Leaving Rome in the general alarm, William went not to Genoa but again to Florence. Having an empty place in the carriage since Sligo's departure, he took with him Charles Fox, son of Lord and Lady Holland, who complained they had no room for him among their numerous retinue. This included a French chef who later in the journey produced an unforgettable dinner on top of the Brenner Pass.

Letter to Sarah.

"Florence, April 26th, 1815. My dear Sarah, - The different exaggerated statements which you have no doubt seen in the newspapers of the state of affairs in Italy have, I fear, given you many needless alarms about my safety. I dread that, in consequence of the difficulty of communication, these too have been greatly augmented, for it

Florence

has been impossible to inform you exactly where I was, what I was doing, nor what were my intentions. Thank God your alarms may now completely cease, for what little danger there might perhaps have existed for us in the southern parts of Italy is now removed since we arrived in Florence, where we are amongst our friends and allies, and where communication with England is perfectly free and open, where there is a British ambassador, and where the most perfect order and tranquillity reign.

The perfect state of ignorance as to public affairs in which we were all kept at Naples inclined us to remain there longer than was, perhaps, altogether prudent. One of the efforts of a despotic government is to prepare its plans with so much secrecy that no one shall have the chance of suspecting them, and so all external communication was cut off, the post was stopped, no foreign newspapers were given out, and the only chance of intelligence which remained was the 'Court Gazette,' which, of course, only gave what was intended to throw dust in our eyes, and to conceal anything likely to arouse our suspicions. The veil was, however, lifted up the moment that the King put himself at the head of his army and invaded the Papal dominion. I took my departure from Naples immediately, with the intention to stay some time in Rome. But during this time the consequences of this rash act of the King began to develop themselves in a way that anyone with the least foresight could have perceived, Never did so rash an act enter into the head of anyone as to imagine that the little state of Naples would be able to contend with the gigantic force of the house of Austria. Could anyone in their senses suppose that an army of 80,000 men, at most, was capable of beating one of a hundred and sixty thousand (the number, at present, of German troops in Italy)? It is true that perhaps the King was led on by false hopes, and flattered himself that Lombardy would rise in his favour, and would catch at the chance of independence and

Florence

liberty, but of this he ought to have assured himself before he hazarded his crown. The chances being so uncertain, he ought to have recollected that though it is very true that the Italians do not like the Austrians, nevertheless the Neapolitans are almost as obnoxious to the rest of Italy, and that he, who proposed himself for their King, was a Frenchman and not an Italian; and further, that the character of the Italian people is much too calculating ever to think of venturing anything, even less of making the smallest sacrifice of any kind whatsoever. They have held fine language about it, but by this he should not have been deceived, for he has now lived long enough in Italy to know how fallacious is all their boasting, and how passive is their submission. He has not profited by his observation, and so he has thrown away a crown which the allies had, I believe, determined at the Congress to confirm to him. His rashness and impetuosity have deprived him of the most beautiful kingdom of the Continent, and nothing but death or captivity now await him. His own troops, too, wherever they have been engaged, no matter how inferior in number was the enemy, have always given way, always been beaten, always been repulsed. Their desertion, too, is enormous; twelve hundred are said to have decamped out of the column of 6,000 which was here, and if this proportion holds good in the main army it will very soon be reduced to the very skeleton and shadow of an army, which cannot possibly stand for an hour against the enormous force which is pouring down upon it.

So much for Italian affairs, which now seem to be finally settled, for I hear this moment that the Neapolitans have been again beaten and with great loss. In a very short time there will be none left to meet the Austrians, who are marching direct upon Naples. The Pope may then return to Rome, as the Grand Duke has here, and all will be quiet again. The Romans and the Tuscans are extremely hostile to the Neapolitans. The peasantry were on

Florence

the point of rising, and it would then indeed have become a national war. It was only at Bologna and one or two other towns that Murat found any friends at all, and then only in very thin numbers, 300, I believe, having subscribed their names at the first place and some few at the others."

On the 30th April Murat's Neapolitan army was routed in the battle of Tolentino. Murat himself reached Naples on 18th May to find it under the control of the Royal Navy. He fled to France the same day, but Napoleon refused his services for the campaign ending at Waterloo. Murat then returned to Calabria where he was captured and executed on 13th October.

"In France, I regret to think, affairs look most gloomy, and I really contemplate them with horror. I cannot yet indeed persuade myself of the facts, and it appears to me as a dream which may still pass away. When I hear, though, of the immense preparations which are making for a second crusade, and think that all the horrors of the year before last are to be renewed, I am horrified. And to think that one individual should cause such misery to so many millions ...

Florence wears at present a very war-like appearance in consequence of the perpetual passage of Austrian troops, which all take the route to Rome. In coming here we have been particularly fortunate, as we just timed it so as not to meet the Neapolitans in their retreat, and consequently we were not delayed a moment, whilst the other English, who ran away as if they were all to be burned the next day, met with every kind of difficulty, and have not been able to advance one step beyond Venice, in consequence of the cold and snow in the Tyrol. I propose to remain here some little time longer, in order to allow the roads to be clear of the troops, and also for the snow to melt before I cross the Alps. I shall then make straight for Munich,

Florence

and so across Germany as circumstances shall direct. I am now writing to Sligo to beg him that he will send all your letters to me at Munich, as being at this moment the only sure point I can fix upon which I am sure to pass through.

Nothing can exceed the beauty of the spring in this delightful valley of the Arno. Everything is now in full beauty - the rains have ceased, the sun is not as yet too powerful ... Many of the English who fled are now returning daily, and I expect Florence will soon be as full of foreigners as ever. My most kind remembrance to all my friends. My best love to my mother and Charlotte. - Your affectionate brother, Wm. Crackanthorpe."

Letter to his mother.

"Florence, May 6th, 1815 My dear Mother, - Just as I am on the point of leaving Florence, I have found an opportunity of sending you a few lines to let you know that I am very well, and also to give you some idea of my movements. The badness of the weather has detained me here for the last fortnight. It has rained incessantly in the valleys and snowed upon the mountains, and even in England I have never experienced a worse season. The last three days, however, have been delicious, and the hay harvest has begun in good earnest. Strawberries we have in abundance and other fruits as well. Tomorrow I set out towards Venice by the route of Ferrara, and I shall thence go direct over the mountains of the Tyrol to Munich, where, I trust, Newbiggin letters will await me.

Affairs in Italy are nearly settled. The present King of Naples cannot hold out much longer. His retreat is cut off, and his soldiers will not fight for him. The moment they come near the enemy they run away, and are not content only to throw away their arms and knapsacks, but even their uniforms, in order that they may run quicker! A person who was at the last action near

Florence

Macurata told me that he never saw such conduct in his life. The officers did their duty, as they were observed actually beating their men on with their swords, and perpetually encouraging them during the attack. I would indeed that the King would surrender. He must now be fully aware that he cannot meet the columns moving on against him, and that he is only prolonging the miseries of war for the sake of preserving a crown which if he does not lose it to-day he must to-morrow. A debarkation is also to take place in Calabria which will very soon settle the whole affair, as Ferdinand, the old King, is to accompany it, and he may march direct to Naples. I am very anxious about the English who are now there, for nothing can be more dreadful than to be in a state of perpetual dread of the rising of the Lazzaroni, and at the same time to be unable to leave the place in consequence of the bands of robbers who infest the road between Naples and Rome.

We are all very anxious to know whether we are to be engaged again in a war with France. The preparations all round make it only too probable, and yet the moderate language of Buonaparte would make one hope that it may be avoided. The real difficulty is, how far it is wise to make peace with a man who never keeps his word. Whatever happens we must hope that war will not again last for 25 years, or we shall be entirely ruined.

I think myself very fortunate in meeting with this opportunity of sending this letter to you. Lord Burgesh's secretary is good enough to detain his courier for me while I actually write it. Best love to Charlotte and Sarah. - Your ever affectionate son, Wm. Crackanthorpe."

Letter to Charlotte.

"Venice, May 22nd, 1815. My dear Charlotte, - I could not pass so near Venice without stopping two or three days to see it again. I am more than ever struck by it … And yet how different is its present condition to

Venice

what it was only 20 years ago —then one of the wealthiest cities, now just as impoverished, its palaces falling in ruins, its pictures stolen, its nobles gone, and a general air of poverty and wretchedness everywhere. No town over the whole Continent has suffered more than Venice.

I am glad to learn that the Viceroy is to be resident here for six months in the year. This will in some degree encourage trade, and so Venice may perhaps not lapse into a neglected provincial town.

A very few days will now finish the campaigning in the south of Italy, as it is utterly impossible that Murat can make any efficient stand at Capua. It is said indeed that the Queen has already capitulated to the English fleet, which is lying in the bay, giving up to it the two ships of the line which were there, and all the stores of the arsenal. So that, if this be true, I think John Bull has already come in for a very pretty share of the booty. The town of Gaita is strong and may hold out for some time, and may thus prevent the Austrian troops from returning to reinforce the army, which is preparing, this side the Alps, to invade France. The preparations for this 19th century crusade are enormous - and how will it all end? Those who have seen the horrors of the last war can never wish to see them all renewed. And yet I fear this is almost inevitable. For my own part I lean strongly to the side of peace. With the internal concerns of any foreign country we have no right to interfere. We must hope that perhaps some desperado may finish what millions are now preparing to fight for, or that the timely hand of death will, in its natural course, cut off this scourge of the world.

I leave for Munich to-morrow. I go first to Verona, thence to Trent, and thence to Insbruck. At Munich I shall find out from our Minister what route it will be best to take for England, whether by the Elbe or by the Rhine, and by his advice I shall

Munich

direct my march. My best love to my mother and Sarah, and believe me your affectionate brother, Wm. Crackanthorpe."

Letter to his mother.
"Munich, June 8th, 1815.
My dearest Mother, - So far am I come on my route home towards England, having passed the great barrier of the Alps, and must confess not without regret. Were it not that I have something much more delightful in view (I mean my own country) I should, I verily believe, return thither. For you can conceive no contrast more striking than that between the Germans and the Italians ... the one with difficulty made to understand your wants, the other performing all your wishes even before you make them known. With all this, though, I must admit that the Germans are an infinitely better sort of people (I do not mean to say more agreeable) and their morality is certainly sounder than that of the inhabitants of the South.

The route from Verona here is really the most beautiful I have seen. It is one delightful picture the whole way. The peasants, too, are here a most interesting race of people, wearing a very picturesque costume. They are exceedingly moral in their habits, most astonishingly attached to their ancient Government, and the joy that they now feel in returning under their ancient Sovereign, the Emperor of Austria, is quite unbounded. Nowhere have I seen a race of people more estimable than these ...

Gigantic war preparations are making all over Germany. Every nerve is stretched to set an army on foot, which shall be at once the largest and best equipped possible. It is hard to believe, but at this moment there are, between the banks of the Don and the Rhine, more than 900,000 men on foot capable of taking part in military service. The same spirit as when I was last here animates the people, and all are ready to meet the foe. The

Munich

Russian army, 250,000 strong, is already in Franconia, and there is no doubt that hostilities will commence very shortly. The two Emperors, - Austria and Russia - passed through here two days before I arrived, and received the warmest welcome. The suite of the Emperor of Russia is quite Asiatic in its number. He has rations ordered daily for fifteen hundred horses and one thousand persons. He has twenty-five generals as aides de camp. It is sad to see the banks of the Rhine completely ruined by the armies, and the greatest misery prevails on all sides. The owners of estates have nothing to live upon. A gentleman here who has one in the Duchy of Baden has received nothing from it for two years past, and, in addition, has had to make contributions as well! Happy ought we to consider ourselves, for though nationally we may be poor, individually we are not, as we are saved from these terrible wars in our own country.

Independent of my desire (no small one) to return to Vienna, which is only two days journey from here, I feel myself obliged to go there to make arrangements with my banker, which I could not make in Italy, for my further homeward progress, So soon, then, as the great personages, such as Prince Metternich and others, who take up all the horses on the road, are passed, I shall set out for Vienna, and shall stay there long enough to hear from you. I shall then go on to Dresden, and then make my way home as quickly as possible. By the month of August, I trust, I shall reach Newbiggin, and find you all well and happy.

I have, I think, no news to tell you. Berthier, as you doubtless know, threw himself out of a window at Hamburg the other day, without any apparent reason."

Marshal Berthier, made Prince of Wagram in 1809, was one of Napoleon's most trusted aides. However, he refused to rejoin Napoleon at the start of the Hundred Days.

"Lord Holland's family arrive here tonight. They are 22 in

Vienna

The Battle of Waterloo, 1815, by William Sadler II

number, which is no bagatelle to move. With my best love to Charlotte and Sarah,

- Your affectionate son, Wm Crackanthorpe."
On June 18th was fought the battle of Waterloo.
Letter to Charlotte.

"Vienna, June 26th, 1815. My dearest Charlotte, - Within three days journey of Vienna how could I resist the temptation of coming hither to see those friends who had been so kind to me on a former occasion! At present, indeed, I find them in a very different state, for the mainspring of their society has been carried off, and their daily point of reunion no longer exists. That they were somewhat prepared, from the age of the old Prince, for his death does not make his loss the less bitter. They are quite an unique family. In none did I ever see a union of so much kindness, goodness and friendship for each other, and at the same time, for all the world. I came here via Salzburg - in my opinion by far the prettiest place in all Germany, its buildings being all admirable and its position amongst the Alps quite unmatched. The Crown Prince of Bavaria has taken up his residence at Salzburg. Unfortunately he was not there or I should certainly have seen him, as he has such an amazing passion for the English. At present Vienna is completely void of all strangers, the members of the Congress being departed and its residents mostly all in the country. A few English, however, still remain, and Mr. Gordon, our charge d'affaires, is, I find, an old college friend of mine. I shall, therefore, stay till I get letters from you, and then set off immediately for England, directing my course by the Pays Bas, which by that time will, I hope, be cleared of troops, as they must have advanced almost to Paris. What a glorious commencement indeed has the first battle been, and under what good auspices do all things seem to be going forward! Thank God, it is a war which must very soon be finished, for the exertions made on all sides are so tremendous that they cannot possibly be continued. It is, indeed, high time, for the hideous and universal misery that reigns throughout every part of the Continent, even among those far removed from the actual seat of war, can only be judged by those who are eye witnesses of it. There is no Government which is not on the point of bankruptcy; and no people that is not in a state of semi-starvation. God grant therefore that this may be the very end of it all. To-morrow I go for two days to Prince Staremberg's place in the country, Dunster by name. The place is interesting to all Englishmen as being the castle in which Richard Coeur de Lion was shut up and kept prisoner for so long on his return from the Holy Land. Give my best love to my mother and Sarah, and believe me, Your affectionate brother, Wm. Crackanthorpe.

On 21st June Napoleon returned to Paris; and on the 22nd he abdicated for the second time.

William to his mother.

"Toplitz, July 12th, 1815.

My dear Mother, - Thus far do I consider myself on my road to England. I shall wait only a few days till I get your letter, for which I have so long looked. I am in serious alarm about you all, so unfortunate have I been on that head, but I trust in Providence that you are well, and that early in September I shall be amongst you all at Newbiggin. Having found a companion in Mr. St. George, an old college friend, we determined to take the route to Prague, and last week we set out. Bohemia, indeed, I had never seen. It is not a very beautiful country, save about its frontiers, but it is, for many reasons, a very interesting one. We are being entertained by the good old Prince Clarig (who married a daughter of the Prince de Ligne) and we could not resist the temptation of accepting his invitation, and seeing how the Germans pass their time and amuse themselves on their estates. Never can I repay this family for all their kindness and goodness to me ...

During the last campaign Dunster was the headquarters of the Sovereigns, and within an hour's ride of it was fought the first battle which turned in the favour of the allies. To-morrow we will go over to Dresden to see the gallery filled with fine pictures. It is one of the few that has escaped the spoliating hand of Napoleon. Dresden is only three posts from here, and the road lies through a most beautiful country, and I look forward greatly to this little expedition. We are all deeply interested in the affairs of France, which do not yet seem by any means concluded. The glory with which Wellington has covered himself is the universal theme of conversation, and you can have no idea how much the

Paris

success of the 18th of June has added to our consideration on the Continent. It is no exaggeration to say that to be an Englishman is now a sufficient passport to be received and courted everywhere.

In a few days we set out for the Rhine. Write to me, therefore, to Brussels (post restante) and send the letters direct, and not through Sligo. This is the only point I can now give you for certain, as I do not yet know whether we shall pass the Rhine at Mayence or at Cologne. Circumstances will guide us. God bless and preserve you all. - Your affectionate son, Wm. Crackanthorpe."

Letter to Sarah, Probably from the Hôtel des Princes where Sligo was installed.

"Rue Richelieu, Aug. 12th, 1815. My dear Sarah, - Eccomi a Parigi, as an Italian would say! This perhaps will surprise you, for when I last wrote I said nothing of this my intention, but when I was at Frankfort finding the road quite open, the posts unmolested, and no difficulties whatever, I thought it was best to take the resolution of coming direct hither instead of going by Brussels and the Pays Bas. I left Toplitz on August 1st, and though I made all haste (without however travelling by night) I did not arrive here till late last evening, so that even now my head still carries the noise of the wheels and the cracking of the postboys' whips. Everything I have found extremely tranquil. I came by the road along which the Russians and Bavarians had marched, and in no one instance have I seen anything which did not prove the most exact and severe discipline. In some of the more remote villages indeed, where detachments had been sent without a superior officer, some small excesses had been committed, but in general the greatest order had been preserved, very much to the credit of the sovereigns

Paris

The Second Capture of Paris by the Allies, 7 July 1815, by G W Terry

and their commanders. But the country everywhere groans under the load of the troops quartered upon it. All the way here from Saarbruck (the frontier town) there is no one single village without a garrison of four men in every house, and the nearer you approach the capital the greater the numbers thus quartered. This alone has, as you may imagine, greatly lowered the spirits of the people, in some they appear to be quite broken, for they have not only to lodge but to feed their guests. And this burden laid upon a people already groaning from the dreadful effects of the last campaign is great indeed. Perhaps the effect will be good, for it must teach them the consequences of ambitious wars, and induce them to accept their present Government. From the provinces indeed there is but one cry, and that is for peace. To live quiet is all they ask, and without troubling themselves who is at the head of the Government (for I have seen very little enthusiasm either for Napoleon or Louis in the country through which I have passed). I cannot pretend to know the feelings of the capital, seeing that I am not yet 24 hours arrived in it.

I trust, though, that their sentiments are similar, and if so, since the point d'appui of all these revolutions no longer exists, peace may prevail and France be at rest.

As a capital I cannot say that Paris strikes me as to compare to London, either for extent, population, or riches. The Strand alone at three o'clock seems to contain more equipages than the whole of Paris, and the shops do not appear to me to be at all so splendid as those of our Metropolis. But in public buildings it far exceeds us both for their number and their beauty. The Tuileries is most magnificent as is the Louvre also. To this last was my first visit, quite early this morning, paid. I flew to make acquaintance with all the fine statues which I had seen replaced by casts only in the Vatican, and the pictures of which only copies remain in the greater part of Italy. Here are all the finest treasures of the world, for every country has been robbed to adorn one gallery, where too many of the most beautiful things are lost from being so ill placed. Imagine a room a quarter of a mile in length (nor do I exaggerate) the walls of which are covered with the chefs d'oeuvre of every school, and the roof supported by columns of the finest marble. But I must not, nor indeed can I enter into any details, as I am still so imperfectly acquainted with it. By next week I shall be able to send you an account of all I see and do. Half England, I understand, is here and the whole is expected by next month! So soon as you receive this write to me addressed Aux Soins de Messrs. Oppermann, Banquiers, Paris. I propose to remain only a fortnight here ... believe me your affectionate brother, Wm. Crackanthorpe.

Paris

My hand shakes yet from being so long in the carriage without using a pen."

Letter to Charlotte.

"Paris, Aug. *25th, 1815.*
My dearest Charlotte, - I am awaiting a letter from Newbiggin with the greatest impatience. I hope you did not neglect to answer the one I wrote you upon my arrival here immediately you got it? As you may conceive, I am most anxious indeed to hear from you, and shall scarcely quit the place before I have allowed a fair time for the going and coming of both letters. By Tuesday this time will have elapsed, and if I do not hear I shall set out for England, taking either the route of Calais or Dieppe. In a week therefore from this I hope to set foot on English ground, and with God's will a very short time afterwards to embrace you all at Newbiggin.

But I must tell you something of my occupation. Paris, then, I think in many respects, the first town in the world. It is inferior to London in riches and above all in cleanliness, but in everything that relates to public establishments it is as superior as possible. To every individual, whatever his tastes, it offers resources perfectly inexhaustible. The man of letters will find in the Library, open to everyone, all the rare manuscripts of the Vatican, and in fact all the other collections of Europe; the man of science and the man of taste find equally inexhaustible fountains. How fortunate I count myself to have come to Paris at a moment when all these things are here. A few days later I should perhaps have found some of the finest pictures removed. In fact every day now fifty or sixty pictures take their departure. Tomorrow it is said that the 'Descent from the Cross,' the second work of art of the kind in the world, will be removed and sent back to Antwerp, whence it came. Thus I have seen what can never be seen again, fore I have found united in one gallery all the chefs d'oeuvre of every country and of every age, and I have had the opportunity of comparing them. I spend all my days thus: My mornings at the galleries; I dine early, ride out with my friend Perceval to the environs (he has his horses here); then I go to the theatre, which is magnificent (if there is anything that pleases), if not we pass the evening together at home.

Of politics I hear next to nothing. We are in the same state of ignorance as the rest of the world. All I know is that for the present all seems quiet, but mystery is the order of the day, and although the Ministers hold conferences the result is never known. Give my best love to my mother and Sarah, - Your affectionate brother, Wm. Crackanthorpe."

Letter to his mother.
"Paris, Sept. 1st, 1815.

My dear Mother, - I have been detained here these two days, there being some difficulty about getting my passports which I had not foreseen. I am now on the point, however, of getting into my carriage to proceed to Brussels to see the plains of Waterloo - the Marathon of our day. By making this little detour (which will not detain me more than a few days) I shall, I think, have seen everything of interest, and, indeed, I should almost be ashamed to return to England without having trodden on the ground .... From Brussels I shall proceed to Ostend, and then embark immediately for England - that blessed country, at present uninfected by the French Revolution ... It is indeed astonishing to compare other countries with her, so much ahead is she in liberty, and in public feeling. Another inducement to me to make this trip is that I have the greatest and most intimate friend I had at Cambridge for my companion, young Broderick. He will accompany me to Brussels, and on to England afterwards.

Yesterday I went over to Malmaison, the residence of the devoted Empress Josephine. It is just like a gentleman's small country house in England outside, but inside are many beautiful pictures. There are four statues by the famous sculptor Canova, which really are equal to the antique. The whole at present belongs to the Empress's son, the Prince Eugene. It is said he means to sell it. It will, I imagine, produce an immense sum, though the pictures are all to go to Munich. By the way, the daily sending off of pictures from the Louvre still goes on. In a short time it will be comparatively bare, and I must say I rejoice with all my heart!

You know far more of public affairs than we do. Indeed, we learn our news from the English papers, which appears odd enough in a city where all the Ministers of all the great Powers are assembled, and in which all the political work is now actually being done. To-morrow I hope to be in Brussels, and to find some of your letters which I have now sought so long, and under this idea, which makes me quite happy, I am, your ever affectionate son, Wm. Crackanthorpe. "

Letter to Sarah.

"Brussels, September 4th, 1815. My dear Sarah, - I arrived here last night, after three days travelling in heat and dust, greater than any I ever experienced, even in Italy. Unfortunately we came along the road occupied by the Prussians, and so could scarcely get anything to eat, much less to eat it with! The conduct of this army is quite unsupportable. They pillage wherever they go, and not content with the food which has been prepared for them, they often go to the length of killing the poor people who have done everything in their power to make them as comfortable as they could, often in a fashion far beyond their means. Consequently the villages

Waterloo

and towns are half deserted, the farmers have left their farms, and thousands are living in the woods as best they can. What will be the end I know not, but I am quite sure that if the other allied armies were not in France, not a single Prussian would leave it alive. I am happy to think that this is not the conduct of our own army, for such is the exactness of their discipline that wherever they go they make themselves respected, and, I may almost say, beloved.

To-morrow we go over the plain of Waterloo, where so many of our brave fellows perished. This is a spot too interesting to be neglected, and though its memories are but too melancholy, nevertheless our nation has there acquired such a name ... that we must feel quite proud. The next day I shall set out for England. I am recommended to go by Calais instead of Ostend ... Brussels appears to me to contain but little of interest. I shall pass through Ghent, and in two days I hope to reach Calais. Write to me at Ibbotson's Hotel in Vere Street, to meet me on my arrival, where I must stay a couple of days to get some clothes made. My best love to you all, je vous embrasse toutes, and may God keep you all. - Your affectionate brother, Wm. Crackanthorpe."

Letter to Charlotte.

"Monday morning, Ibbotson's Hotel. My dear Charlotte, - After having been shaken to death upon the pavement all the way from Brussels to Calais, I embarked there on Saturday morning, and my usual ill luck at sea pursuing me, had a calm so dead that we could not arrive until Sunday, instead of doing the journey in two and a half hours, which is the ordinary passage. I am, now, however, arrived in London, and find myself almost without clothes, as I have had nothing made for me since I went out, except one coat. I shall, therefore, have to wait here two or three days to get myself a coat and some shoes, in fact the indispensable.

I am also without a servant, William Macintosh having conducted himself so ill at Paris that I am determined to keep him no longer. I am, therefore, looking out for another, and this, too, may detain me for a few days. London is more deserted than any town in Italy. I will write you by the mail on Thursday to inform you of the day of my departure. I have no news save that the people of the Pays Bas are very discontented, and that things on the Continent are going as well as possible.

I cannot tell you the delight with which I hailed the white cliffs of this dear country. This pleasure can only be exceeded by embracing you all at Newbiggin ... I am only just in time to save the post. Your affectionate brother, Wm. Crackanthorpe."

Epilogue

After an absence of more than three years, William now turned his attention to the management and repair of the Newbiggin estate, the farm houses and buildings, the woodlands and eventually of the Hall itself. His diaries, especially those written during the Irish tour, show his belief in the value for rural communities of the permanent presence of a dutiful landowner. His admiration for Sir Edward O'Brien's work at Dromoland is the chief example. Newbiggin estate accounts have not survived but it is known that after 1815 all the farm houses were rebuilt and reconstruction was done in the interior of that part of the Hall where the single-storied dining hall of 1533 had stood. William had also in prospect the rebuilding of the damaged West tower at Newbiggin, eventually to be carried out to designs by Anthony Salvin, turning at least a part of the ancient edifice into a comfortable, modernised home within the walls of a mediaeval tower house. And the church awaited restoration. Meanwhile, sale of isolated parcels of land and acquisition of others resulted in a modest, slow increase in the acreage of the estate.

After so much travelling, William may have found his wanderlust appeased, and that the attachment to Newbiggin which was to be the leading feature of his life had overtaken it, though he continued his visits to London and, in this early period, to Bute where Raeburn's portrait, now in Dumfries House, was painted in 1820.

William lived to 98. Regrettably few records of this long life have survived. He may have destroyed his correspondence, or this may have been done by his heir and successor at Newbiggin,

Montague Crackanthorpe. He had many friends, and the evidence of the "forty letters and ten folded notes, mostly from young ladies" found with his diaries, suggests that he had, at least as a young man, a lively interest in the possibilities of love life. Yet he never married, nor did his sisters. For him, at least, there must have been adventures to follow the normal experiences of a Grand Tourist circling continental capitals. Family belief was that William was in love for years with Lady Hatherton, wife of the politician who, as Edward Littleton, was Irish Secretary in Lord Grey's Whig Government. William was certainly guardian to her son by her first marriage, Arthur Bromley Davenport of Capesthorne, during his minority, and her marble bust stood in the library of the Salvin tower at Newbiggin. If the family was right, this would have meant either a frustrating long term experience from which relief was probably found in London, or a clandestine relationship liable at any time to painful and expensive collapse. The outcome, for William, was a seemingly uneventful emotional life into which he settled with his memories, relying on friendships and the love he had for his home and his counties of origin. But such a long, calm summer and autumn of life could very well, in 19th century fashion, have masked other unrecorded episodes when restrictive habits were eased —or left to others.

In 1826 William was High Sheriff of Cumberland, and from 1830 he was magistrate in both counties by appointment of Lord Brougham, now Lord Chancellor in the first Whig Government since 1806. He continued active as a Whig in local politics but after failing to be elected in 1832 he appears to have withdrawn from the quest of a local seat in Tory country. And so strong was his local attachment, and his commitment to the ideal of the landowner's presence, that it is very unlikely he would ever have been tempted to look for nomination in any other part of the country. The Eden Valley and its surrounding fells imprint a loyalty in the Cumbrian psyche. He restored the church, built and endowed a Sunday School in Newbiggin village, built a teacher's house adjoining it, as well as a number of others, and endowed scholarships to carry any promising local boy on into further education. He was Deputy Lieutenant of Westmorland, and from 1834 to 1874 chairman of the Board of Guardians in Westmorland under the Poor Law Amendment Act of the Whig Government of Lord Grey. In short, he lived as a country squire was expected to live, but at the expense of the more fulfilling career which, as a young man, he might have imagined. If this was a disappointment, then almost a century of peace, of watching the growth of trees and the productivity of land, was the recompense.

And though few records remain, there was of course the active social life which certainly didn't come to an end in 1815. For example his friendly relations with Lord and Lady Holland, formed in the Alps, made him a seasonal familiar at gatherings in the Whig social centre of Holland House in Kensington. The first mention of his name in the Holland House Dinner Books seems to be on June 5th 1818; also present were Henry Brougham and Sydney Smith, founding editors of the famous Whig-supporting *Edinburgh Review,* and Lord Morpeth, later Earl of Carlisle and a confirmed Whig.

When Lord Sligo returned to Ireland, he devoted himself fully to care and development of his property and reordering of his finances at Westport, to Irish political affairs, and to a career of race horse breeding in which he was notably successful. He married and fathered fourteen children by his wife who was sixteen at the birth of the first of them, and the marriage seems to have been entirely happy. Sligo's move from an inherited Toryism towards more liberal policies was marked by his support

Newbiggin Hall, 1840

Newbiggin Hall, Salvin tower, 1844

Sligoville in Jamaica and the sign outside the village

for Henry Brougham's campaign in favour of the Reform Act of 1832; and by his own efforts in aid of the Irish population during the famine of those years. From inheritance through the Kelly family, he was owner of plantations in Jamaica, with 586 slaves. Perhaps as a known supporter by now of Henry Brougham, the most passionate and eloquent of abolitionists, Sligo was appointed Governor General of Jamaica in August 1833, a month after the passing of the Abolition of Slavery Act through Parliament; and he continued in office until 1836. Slavery was replaced under the Act not by full freedom, but by a system of enforced apprenticeship which became the particular target of the abolitionists of the Anti-Slavery Society, with Sligo prominent

Willliam Crackanthorpe by George Howard, 1877.

among them. On 22 March 1838 he announced in the House of Lords his intention to emancipate all apprentices on his Jamaican estates on 1st August, a decision credited with immense importance in the struggle against plantation owners' interests and powers in the island. Sligo's name as 'the emancipator of the slaves' is celebrated in the town of Sligoville, reputed as the first Free Village in Jamaica. He died at the early age of 62 in January, 1845.

In later life William's principal friendships in Cumbria were with the Howard family, at Greystoke and at Naworth. Esme Howard (1st Lord Howard of Penrith) wrote of his and his brothers' youth at Greystoke in the 1860s and '70s that "Beyond close cousins and one or two old friends of my father's, such as old Mr. Philip Howard of Corby ... Mr.Charles Howard, of Naworth ... Sir Henry Howard, British Minister at Munich, and old Mr. Crackenthorpe, of Newbiggin Hall, no one came to disturb our family party. Mr. Crackenthorpe was born in the eighteenth century and told me once that the pleasantest parties he remembered in Florence as a young man were those given by the Comtesse d'Albany, widow of Prince Charles Edward, the 'Young Pretender.'"

In 1877 the artist George Howard (9th Earl of Carlisle from 1889) made a pencil and crayon portrait of William at Naworth which shows a man not discontent with his life of already 87 years, at ease in a familiar world and immersed in a book. The inelegant discomforts of old age, with failing light and dying sound, seem still far distant.